These tell y[...]
are clues fo[...]
 There are [...]
Flip Quiz a[...]
a vast range of questions about
everything to do with the movies.

This is how to use your *Flip Quiz at the Movies*. If you are answering questions on your own just cover the answers with your hand or a piece of card. You may want to write down your answers and count up your scores for each quiz.

If you are doing the quizzes with a partner or in teams, unfold the base and stand the *Flip Quiz at the Movies* on a flat surface between you and your partner. Read aloud the questions (but not the answers!) and allow your partner to say the answers or write them down. You may answer each question in turn or answer an entire quiz in turn. Keep your scores on a piece of paper and compare results.

The illustrations are there to help you get the right answers when competing with a partner. For instance, if you are answering Quiz 1 questions, you will be looking at and reading out Quiz 2. However, the illustrations you will see are clues to help you do Quiz 1. Look at the labels by the illustrations.

Headings
Look out for specialist subjects, general questions and special quizzes for the younger movie enthusiasts

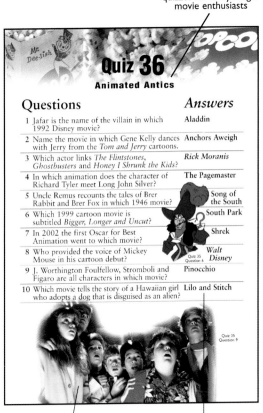

Quiz 36
Animated Antics

Questions	Answers
1 Jafar is the name of the villain in which 1992 Disney movie?	Aladdin
2 Name the movie in which Gene Kelly dances with Jerry from the *Tom and Jerry* cartoons.	Anchors Aweigh
3 Which actor links *The Flintstones*, *Ghostbusters* and *Honey I Shrunk the Kids*?	Rick Moranis
4 In which animation does the character of Richard Tyler meet Long John Silver?	The Pagemaster
5 Uncle Remus recounts the tales of Brer Rabbit and Brer Fox in which 1946 movie?	Song of the South
6 Which 1999 cartoon movie is subtitled *Bigger, Longer and Uncut*?	South Park
7 In 2002 the first Oscar for Best Animation went to which movie?	Shrek
8 Who provided the voice of Mickey Mouse in his cartoon debut?	Walt Disney
9 J. Worthington Foulfellow, Stromboli and Figaro are all characters in which movie?	Pinocchio
10 Which movie tells the story of a Hawaiian girl who adopts a dog that is disguised as an alien?	Lilo and Stitch

Quiz 35 Question 6

Quiz 35 Question 9

Picture clues
These visual clues will often help you get the answer – the label tells you which question they refer to

Answers
When doing the quizzes on your own, cover the answers with your hand or a piece of card

Quiz 1

Lights, Camera, Action

Questions	Answers
1 In which movie does Tom Hanks play a prison guard called Paul Edgecomb?	**The Green Mile**
2 Who has played the Prince of Wales, Charlie Chan and Hercule Poirot?	*Peter Ustinov*
3 In which capital city was the actor Russell Crowe born?	*Wellington*
4 Which heart-throb actor plays the father of the spy kids in the movie of the same name?	*Antonio Banderas*
5 Who played the title role in the epic movie *Spartacus*?	*Kirk Douglas*
6 What was Billy Crystal's profession in the comedy *Analyze This*?	*Psychiatrist*
7 Who played Morpheus in the futuristic thriller *The Matrix*?	*Laurence Fishburne*
8 What is the title of the third in the series of *Austin Powers* movies?	**Goldmember**
9 Which 1964 movie tells the story of an 1879 battle fought in Africa?	**Zulu**
10 Which medieval author was portrayed by Paul Bettany in the movie *The Knight's Tale*?	*Geoffrey Chaucer*

Quiz 2
Question 5

Quiz 2
Question 1

Quiz 2

The Director's Cut

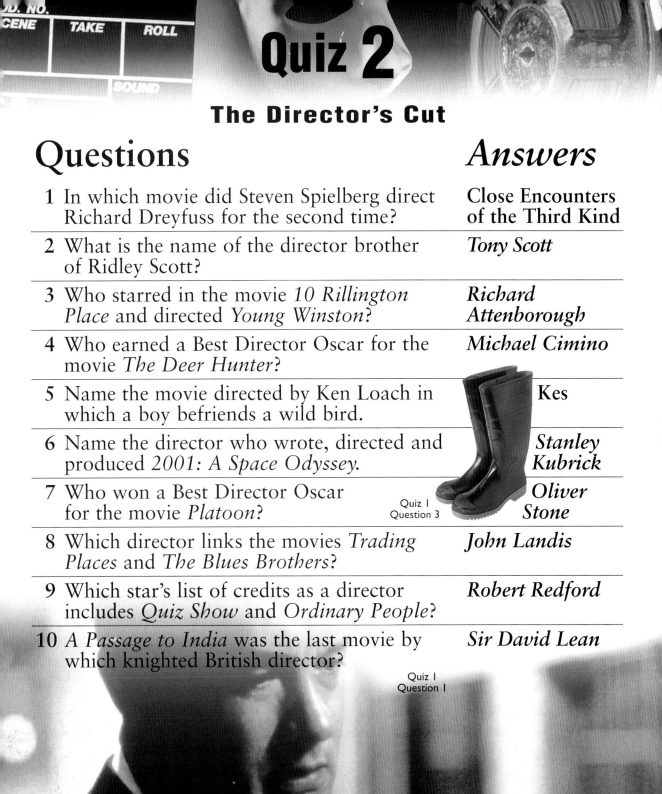

Questions	Answers
1 In which movie did Steven Spielberg direct Richard Dreyfuss for the second time?	**Close Encounters of the Third Kind**
2 What is the name of the director brother of Ridley Scott?	*Tony Scott*
3 Who starred in the movie *10 Rillington Place* and directed *Young Winston*?	**Richard Attenborough**
4 Who earned a Best Director Oscar for the movie *The Deer Hunter*?	*Michael Cimino*
5 Name the movie directed by Ken Loach in which a boy befriends a wild bird.	**Kes**
6 Name the director who wrote, directed and produced *2001: A Space Odyssey*.	*Stanley Kubrick*
7 Who won a Best Director Oscar for the movie *Platoon*?	*Oliver Stone*
8 Which director links the movies *Trading Places* and *The Blues Brothers*?	*John Landis*
9 Which star's list of credits as a director includes *Quiz Show* and *Ordinary People*?	*Robert Redford*
10 *A Passage to India* was the last movie by which knighted British director?	*Sir David Lean*

Quiz I
Question 3

Quiz I
Question I

Quiz 3
Bond, James Bond

Questions	Answers
1 What item of attire did the Bond villain Oddjob use as a lethal weapon?	*A bowler hat*
2 Who played the bride of James Bond in the movie *On Her Majesty's Secret Service*?	*Diana Rigg*
3 In which movie did 007 kill an agent called Red Grant aboard a train?	**From Russia with Love**
4 Who made her last appearance as Miss Moneypenny in *A View to a Kill*?	*Lois Maxwell*
5 Hugo Drax was the villain in which Bond movie?	**Moonraker**
6 Who sang the theme song for *Thunderball*?	*Tom Jones*
7 On which Caribbean island did Ian Fleming write the *James Bond* novels?	*Jamaica*
8 In which movie did the Israeli actor Topol play a Greek smuggler called Columbo?	**For Your Eyes Only**
9 The title of which Bond movie is also James Bond's family motto?	**The World is Not Enough**
10 Which Scottish actor played a gangland boss called Valentin Zukovsky in two movies?	*Robbie Coltrane*

Quiz 4
Question 4

Quiz 4
Question 9

Quiz 4

The Wild, Wild, West

Questions	Answers
1 Which historical figure did Richard Widmark play in the *The Alamo*?	*Jim Bowie*
2 In which 1952 classic western did Gary Cooper star as Will Kane?	**High Noon**
3 Chris, Vin, Bernardo, Lee, Harry, Britt and Chico are collectively known as who?	**The Magnificent Seven**
4 In which comedy western did Kevin Kline play dual roles?	**Wild, Wild West**
5 Name Emilio Estevez's brother who co-starred with him in the movie *Young Guns*.	*Charlie Sheen*
6 In which spoof western directed by Mel Brooks did Gene Wilder play the Waco Kid?	**Blazing Saddles**
7 Who played Liberty Valance in *The Man Who Shot Liberty Valance*?	*Lee Marvin*
8 In which movie did Alan Ladd proclaim, "A man's gotta do what a man's gotta do"?	*Shane*
9 Kurt Russell played the lawman Wyatt Earp in which movie western?	Tombstone
10 Who played Mel Gibson's father in the comedy western *Maverick*?	*James Garner*

Quiz 3
Question 1

Quiz 3
Question 8

Quiz 5
Name That Year

Questions	Answers
1 *Dirty Dancing, Fatal Attraction* and *Wall Street*	1987
2 *Gladiator, Mission Impossible II* and *The Perfect Storm*	2000
3 *Cool Hand Luke, The Graduate* and *The Dirty Dozen*	1967
4 *Shampoo, Jaws* and *Monty Python and the Holy Grail*	1975
5 *The Hunt For Red October, Pretty Woman* and *Goodfellas*	1990
6 *Lady and the Tramp, Rebel Without a Cause* and *The Seven Year Itch*	1955
7 *Raiders of the Lost Ark, Arthur* and *Chariots of Fire*	1981
8 *The Lion King, Speed* and *True Lies*	1994
9 *Love Story, Patton* and *Woodstock*	1970
10 *Jerry Maguire, Scream* and *Trainspotting*	1996

Quiz 6
Question 3

Quiz 6
Question 8

Quiz 6
Name That Film

Questions	Answers
1 1968 – Steve McQueen, Faye Dunaway, Yaphet Kotto and Paul Burke	The Thomas Crown Affair
2 1993 – Robert Redford, Woody Harrelson Demi Moore and Billy Connolly	Indecent Proposal
3 1991 – Kevin Costner, Gary Oldman, Joe Pesci and John Candy	JFK
4 1993 – Sylvester Stallone, Wesley Snipes, Sandra Bullock and Nigel Hawthorne	Demolition Man
5 1956 – Charlton Heston, Yul Brynner, Vincent Price and Edward G. Robinson	The Ten Commandments
6 1959 – Tony Curtis, Jack Lemmon, Marilyn Monroe and George Raft	Some Like It Hot
7 1995 – Johnny Depp, Christina Ricci, Michael Gambon and Christopher Lee	Sleepy Hollow
8 1945 – Elizabeth Taylor, Mickey Rooney, Donald Crisp and Angela Lansbury	National Velvet
9 1964 – Julie Andrews, Dick Van Dyke, David Tomlinson and Glynis Johns	Mary Poppins
10 1996 – Geoffrey Rush, John Gielgud, Lynn Redgrave and Googie Withers	Shine

Quiz 5
Question 2

Quiz 7

Disney Delights

Questions	Answers
1 *Return to Neverland* was a belated sequel to which Disney classic?	Peter Pan
2 In the movie *Gremlins* which Disney picture did the gremlins watch in a cinema?	Snow White and the Seven Dwarfs
3 Which movie features the song "I've got no Strings"?	Pinocchio
4 Who did Demi Moore voice in the movie *The Hunchback of Notre Dame*?	*Esmerelda*
5 Which classic novel was the subject of Disney's first live action feature in 1950?	Treasure Island
6 What kind of birds are John, Paul, George and Ringo in *The Jungle Book*?	*Vultures*
7 Musafa is the ruler of Pride Rock in which Disney animation?	The Lion King
8 Which Disney movie features the characters of Trixie, Henry, Zeb, Fred and Ted?	The Country Bears
9 Which Disney movie features a crab called Sebastian?	The Little Mermaid
10 The song "You'll be in my Heart" won a Best Song Oscar for which Disney movie?	Tarzan

Quiz 8
Question 5

Quiz 8

Star Wars – May The Force Be With You!

Questions	Answers
1 What kind of creature is Chewbacca?	Wookie
2 Who was the apprentice of the Jedi knight Qui-Gon Jinn?	Obi-Wan Kenobi
3 Which small furry forest dwellers live on Endor?	Ewoks
4 What is the title of the fifth movie to be made in the *Star Wars* series?	Attack of the Clones
5 What is the name of the slug gangster that froze Han Solo in *The Empire Strikes Back*?	Jabba the Hutt
6 Which revered Jedi master spent his final years living on the planet of Dagobah?	Yoda
7 Luke Skywalker lived on which planet before becoming a Jedi knight?	Tatooine
8 Organa is the last name of which *Star Wars* character?	Princess Leia
9 What was Darth Vader called before he turned to the dark side?	Anakin Skywalker
10 Which actor voiced Darth Vader in *Star Wars*?	James Earl Jones

Quiz 7
Question 6

Quiz 7
Question 1

Quiz 9

In The Beginning – The Early Years Of Film

Questions	Answers
1 Who starred in the 1927 movie *The Jazz Singer*?	*Al Jolson*
2 Which silent movie star has a statue in Leicester Square, London?	*Charlie Chaplin*
3 What was the first name of the comedy actor "Fatty" Arbuckle?	*Roscoe*
4 Which legendary screen lover starred in *The Sheik* and *The Eagle*?	*Rudolph Valentino*
5 Which silent movie star was dubbed "Great Stone Face" as he never smiled on screen?	*Buster Keaton*
6 What were early cinemas called in the U.S.A., because the entry fee was five cents?	*Nickelodeon*
7 Which manic police force made their screen debut in a 1912 movie *Hoffmeyer's Legacy*?	*The Keystone Kops*
8 Who was born Arthur Stanley Jefferson?	*Stan Laurel*
9 Which actress played opposite the giant gorilla in the original version of *King Kong*?	*Fay Wray*
10 In what decade were the Oscars first awarded?	*1920s*

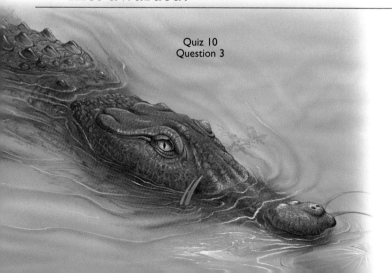

Quiz 10
Question 3

Quiz 10
Question 7

Horror – Scream And Scream Again!

Questions	Answers
1 Which 2002 movie sees David Arquette battling against giant spiders?	Eight Legged Freaks
2 In *The Shining* Jack Nicholson fell into madness while staying at which hotel?	*Overlook Hotel*
3 What type of creature eats its way through the cast in the 1999 movie *Lake Placid*?	*Crocodile*
4 Which serial killer was featured in the 1974 movie *The Texas Chainsaw Massacre*?	*Ed Gein*
5 When Gary Oldman played Count Dracula, who played Van Helsing?	*Anthony Hopkins*
6 Name the actor who played Freddie Krueger in the *Nightmare On Elm Street* movies.	**Robert Englund**
7 Michael Myers is the name of the killer in which series of horror movies?	Halloween
8 Which star of the TV sitcom *Friends* played reporter Gale Weathers in the *Scream* movies?	*Courtney Cox*
9 Who has been played on screen by Kenneth Branagh and Peter Cushing?	*Baron Frankenstein*
10 Who played Rosemary in the movie *Rosemary's Baby*?	*Mia Farrow*

Quiz 9
Question 2

Quiz 9
Question 4

Quiz 11
Choc Ices – For The Kids

Questions	Answers
1 Are E.T.'s eyes green, blue, brown or yellow?	*Blue*
2 Which animated duo are particularly fond of Wensleydale cheese?	*Wallace and Gromit*
3 In the movie *Home Alone* what is the first name of the boy left home alone?	*Kevin*
4 What kind of animal is Rocky in *The Adventures of Rocky and Bullwinkle*?	*Squirrel*
5 Which movie features the characters of Fred, Velma, Daphne, Shaggy and a talking dog?	Scooby-Doo
6 What is the name of the piggybank in *Toy Story*?	*Hamm*
7 Which 2000 animated movie sees Emperor Kuzco transformed into a llama?	The Emperor's New Groove
8 In the movie *Dinosaur* what is the name of the leader of the dinosaurs?	*Kron*
9 Is the family cat in the movie *Stuart Little*, black, white or tortoiseshell?	*White*
10 In which movie is Bugs Bunny assisted by basketball superstar Michael Jordan?	Space Jam

Quiz 12
Question 5

Quiz 12

Hot Dogs – For The Kids

Questions	Answers
1 In which movie does a sheep dog called Fly become a foster parent to a pig?	Babe
2 What type of animal was voiced by Eddie Murphy in the movie *Shrek*?	Donkey
3 Who stole Christmas in a 2000 movie?	The Grinch
4 In the movie *Johnny Neutron* what piece of kitchen equipment is made into a satellite?	Toaster
5 What kind of animal is Bullwinkle in *The Adventures of Rocky and Bullwinkle*?	Moose
6 What is the name of Sid's dog in *Toy Story*?	Scud
7 Which movie features a hen called Ginger and farm owners called Mr. and Mrs. Tweedy?	Chicken Run
8 In the movie *A Bug's Life* Flik hires circus performers to defend his colony from what?	Grasshoppers
9 Manfred, Sid and Diego are all characters in which movie?	Ice Age
10 What's the name of the bear who befriends Mowgli in *The Jungle Book*?	Baloo

Quiz 11
Question 9

Quiz 11
Question 4

Quiz 13
Heroes And Villains

Questions	Answers
1 Which actor plays Agent K in the *Men in Black* movies?	*Tommy Lee Jones*
2 Which horror movie legend played the abominable *Dr. Phibes* in two movies?	*Vincent Price*
3 Which super villain is played by Willem Dafoe in the 2002 movie *Spiderman?*	*The Green Goblin*
4 Who played the heroic *Condorman* in the 1981 Disney production?	*Michael Crawford*
5 Which actress had a fatal attraction for Michael Douglas?	*Glenn Close*
6 In which action thriller did the hero and villain exchange identities?	*Face/Off*
7 Which Irish actor played the devil in the movie *End of Days?*	*Gabriel Byrne*
8 Who played the father of Indiana Jones in *Indiana Jones and the Last Crusade*?	*Sean Connery*
9 Which Bond villain was played by Joseph Wiseman?	*Dr. No*
10 Who played the title role in the 1984 movie *Supergirl*?	*Helen Slater*

Quiz 14
Question 6

Quiz 14
Question 4

Quiz 14
Cops And Robbers

Questions	Answers
1 Who played Mel Gibson's partner in the *Lethal Weapon* movies?	*Danny Glover*
2 Which Bond movie tells of a plot to rob Fort Knox?	Goldfinger
3 Which 1989 movie starred Tom Hanks as a detective with a large dog for a partner?	Turner and Hooch
4 Which 1963 criminal event was chronicled in the 1988 movie *Buster*?	*The Great Train Robbery*
5 Who played Inspector Dreyfus in the *Pink Panther* movies?	*Herbert Lom*
6 Which series of movies featured a wisecracking cop called Axel Foley?	**Beverly Hills Cop**
7 Who played Detective Jack Cates in the movie *48 Hours*?	*Nick Nolte*
8 In which movie did Sylvester Stallone play the sheriff of a small New Jersey town?	Cop Land
9 In which country did *Butch Cassidy and the Sundance Kid* meet a violent death?	*Bolivia*
10 Who played opposite Sean Connery in the movie *Entrapment*?	*Catherine Zeta Jones*

Quiz 13
Question 5

Quiz 15

War Films – Battle Stations

Questions	Answers
1 Which movie about an army DJ was based on the life of Adrian Cronauer?	Good Morning Vietnam
2 Who refused an Oscar for his 1970 portrayal of General Patton?	*George C. Scott*
3 Who played Private Ryan in the movie *Saving Private Ryan*?	*Matt Damon*
4 In which movie did Burt Lancaster enjoy a steamy love scene with Deborah Kerr?	From Here to Eternity
5 Which 1957 movie told the story of British soldiers forced to build a bridge?	Bridge on the River Kwai
6 In which country were the fields in the 1984 movie *The Killing Fields*?	*Cambodia*
7 In which movie did Tom Cruise play Vietnam veteran Ron Kovic?	Born on the Fourth of July
8 Set in the Korean War, which movie features the characters of Hotlips and Hawkeye?	M*A*S*H
9 Which movie told the true story of a mission into Somalia by 123 U.S. soldiers?	Black Hawk Down
10 Name the movie in which Mel Gibson and Robert Downey Jr. played a pair of pilots.	Air America

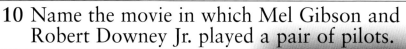

Quiz 16
Question 4

Quiz 16
Question 1

Quiz 16

The Godfather

Questions	Answers
1 Who refused the Best Actor Oscar for his role in *The Godfather*?	*Marlon Brando*
2 Who played the role of Michael Corleone in all three movies?	*Al Pacino*
3 Which actor played the role of Sonny Corleone, Michael's brother?	*James Caan*
4 In the movies, Johnny Fontane was said to have been inspired by which singer?	*Frank Sinatra*
5 Who directed *The Godfather* movies?	*Francis Ford Coppola*
6 Which word beginning with M was omitted deliberately from the screenplay of the movies?	*Mafia*
7 Which actor played Tom Hagen, the legal advisor to the Corleone family?	*Robert Duvall*
8 Which actress played the role of Kay Adams and the title role in the movie *Annie Hall*?	*Diane Keaton*
9 On whose novel was *The Godfather* based?	*Mario Puzo*
10 Who played Michael's sister Connie and went on to play the wife of Rocky Balboa?	*Talia Shire*

Quiz 15
Question 6

Quiz 15
Question 1

Quiz 17

In The Foyer – General

Questions	Answers
1 Who played the boss of Julia Roberts in the movie *Erin Brockovich*?	*Albert Finney*
2 The Palme d'Or is the top award at which movie festival?	*Cannes*
3 Who played the role of Professor Xavier in the movie *X-Men*?	*Patrick Stewart*
4 Which movie was set in Dublin and featured the song "Mustang Sally"?	**The Commitments**
5 Who played Count Dracula for the last time in the movie *The Satanic Rites of Dracula*?	*Christopher Lee*
6 Which heavyweight boxing champion had a cameo role in the 2001 movie *Ocean's Eleven*?	*Lennox Lewis*
7 Who played the title role in the movie *Edward Scissorhands*?	*Johnny Depp*
8 In which movie did Richard Attenborough play a millionaire called John Hammond?	**Jurassic Park**
9 Which movie star is the daughter of Tippi Hendren, and the ex-wife of Don Johnson?	*Melanie Griffith*
10 Which song was performed by the cast at the beginning of the movie *Grease*?	*"Summer Nights"*

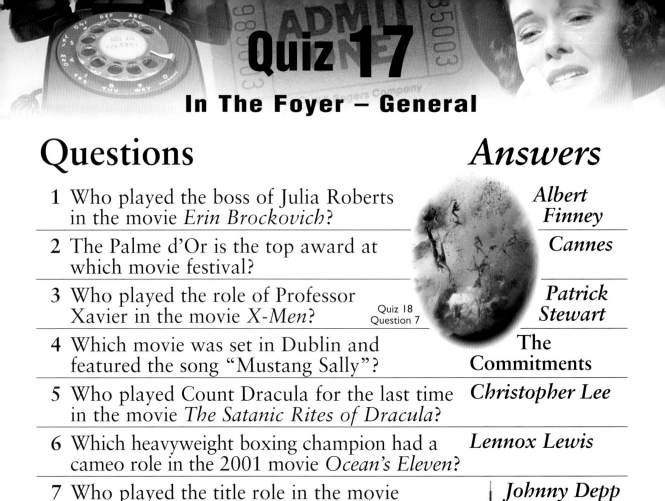

Quiz 18
Question 7

Quiz 18
Question 8

Quiz 18
Matinee – General

Questions	Answers
1 Which British actor played the husband of Geena Davis in the movie *Stuart Little*?	*Hugh Laurie*
2 In which movie was Samuel L. Jackson devoured by a super-intelligent shark?	Deep Blue Sea
3 In which movie did Russell Crowe play schizophrenic mathematician John Nash?	A Beautiful Mind
4 Who provided the voice of Jessica Rabbit in the movie *Who Framed Roger Rabbit*?	*Kathleen Turner*
5 The character of Austin Powers featured in the video for which Madonna song?	"Beautiful Stranger"
6 The 2001 film *Iris* chronicled the life of which writer?	*Iris Murdoch*
7 What natural disaster did Pierce Brosnan combat in the movie *Dante's Peak*?	*A volcanic eruption*
8 In which city is the movie *Moulin Rouge* set?	*Paris*
9 Which star of *Gone with the Wind* was known as the "King of Hollywood"?	*Clark Gable*
10 Which British actor played Boromir in *The Lord of the Rings*?	*Sean Bean*

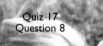

Quiz 17
Question 8

Quiz 19
Fred Astaire

Questions	Answers
1 In which century was Astaire born?	*19th century – born in 1899*
2 The song "White Christmas" featured in which movie starring Astaire and Crosby?	Holiday Inn
3 What was the title of the 1936 movie in which Astaire played a sailor on shore leave?	Follow the Fleet
4 What name was he born with?	*Frederick Austerlitz*
5 Which movie features the song "Dancing Cheek to Cheek"?	Top Hat
6 What is the name of Astaire's sister, who was also his first dancing partner?	*Adele*
7 In which movie did he receive an Oscar nomination for his role as a conman?	The Towering Inferno
8 His first movie starring with Ginger Rogers was called *Flying Down to* where?	Rio
9 In the movie *Easter Parade*, Astaire played Don Hewes. Who played Hannah Brown?	Judy Garland
10 In what year of the 1980s did Astaire die?	*1987*

Quiz 20
Question 8

Quiz 20

Judy Garland

Questions	Answers
1 What was the first name of Judy's character in *The Wizard of Oz*?	*Dorothy*
2 Which 1964 movie co-starring Judy chronicled the 1948 Nazi War Trials?	**Judgment at Nuremberg**
3 Which director was she married to from 1945 to 1961?	*Vincente Minnelli*
4 Which diminutive actor was Judy's co-star in ten movies from 1938 to 1948?	*Mickey Rooney*
5 In which movie did Judy sing "The Trolley Song"?	**Meet Me in St. Louis**
6 What was the name given to Judy when she was born?	*Frances Gumm*
7 How many times did she marry?	*Five times*
8 In which 1954 movie did James Mason play Judy's alcoholic husband?	**A Star is Born**
9 What is the name of her youngest daughter who also performs as a singer?	*Lorna Luft*
10 In what year of the 1960s did Judy die, a few weeks after her 47th birthday?	*1969*

Quiz 19
Question 5

Quiz 19
Question 9

Quiz 21

Front Row Seats – General

Questions	Answers
1 In which country was *The Lord of the Rings* trilogy filmed?	*New Zealand*
2 Which star of the sitcom *Cheers* featured in the movie *Three Men and a Baby*?	*Ted Danson*
3 Which famous model played the leading lady in *The Boy Friend*?	*Twiggy*
4 What is the name of the acting brother of Jeff Bridges?	*Beau Bridges*
5 Who links the movies *Seven, Along Came a Spider* and *The Shawshank Redemption*?	*Morgan Freeman*
6 Which superstar singer played Breathless Mahoney in *Dick Tracy*?	*Madonna*
7 What is the favourite food of the Teenage Mutant Ninja Turtles?	*Pizza*
8 Which *James Bond* comedy co-starred David Niven, Peter Sellers and Woody Allen?	**Casino Royale**
9 Which pretty woman married Danny Moder in July 2002?	*Julia Roberts*
10 Which actor starred in and directed the comedy *Zoolander*?	*Ben Stiller*

Quiz 22
Question 10

Quiz 22
Preview – General

Questions	Answers
1 Who has Paul Newman been married to since 1958?	*Joanne Woodward*
2 Which British comedy star played the title role in *The Parole Officer*?	*Steve Coogan*
3 In 2002 which Hollywood star announced he was suffering from Alzheimer's disease?	*Charlton Heston*
4 Who played the New York cop Popeye Doyle in two movies?	*Gene Hackman*
5 Which actor was forced to take a lie detector test in the 2000 comedy *Meet the Parents*?	*Ben Stiller*
6 Which movie co-starring Robert Carlyle and Samuel L. Jackson is set in Liverpool?	**The 51st State**
7 Name the actress who played the wife of Kevin Spacey in *American Beauty*.	*Annette Bening*
8 Who played the C.I.A. operative Jack Ryan in the 2002 movie *The Sum of all Fears*?	*Ben Affleck*
9 Who played the leading lady in *What Women Want* and *As Good as it Gets*?	*Helen Hunt*
10 Name the baby in the 2002 movie *Monsters Inc*.	*Boo*

Quiz 23

Sci-Fi

Questions	Answers
1 Who played Rebecca Howe in the sitcom *Cheers* and Lieutenant Saavik in *Star Trek II*?	*Kirstie Alley*
2 In which American city was the Ridley Scott sci-fi thriller *Bladerunner* set?	*Los Angeles*
3 Which H.G. Wells novel was first filmed in 1960 starring Rod Taylor?	The Time Machine
4 In which movie were senior citizens rejuvenated by extra-terrestrial powers?	Cocoon
5 Name the 1997 sci-fi action thriller that starred Bruce Willis and Gary Oldman.	The Fifth Element
6 In which movie were John Hurt and Sigourney Weaver crewmates aboard a spacecraft?	Alien
7 Who played the time traveller Dr. Emmett Brown in the *Back to the Future* movies?	*Christopher Lloyd*
8 Which droid spoke the first line of dialogue in the movie *Star Wars*?	*C-3PO*
9 Name Dennis Quaid's brother who starred in the movie *Independence Day*.	*Randy Quaid*
10 In which movie did Jack Nicholson play President Dale?	Mars Attacks

Quiz 24
Question 9

Quiz 24
Question 5

Questions

1 Who composed the music for the spaghetti western *The Good, the Bad and the Ugly*?

2 Who sang "Beauty School Dropout" on the soundtrack of the musical *Grease*?

3 Which king of ragtime music featured in the Oscar-winning movie *The Sting*?

4 Who wrote the songs for the musical *Oliver*?

5 Which soundtrack featured Whitney Houston singing "I'm Every Woman"?

6 Mike Oldfield's "Tubular Bells" featured in which horror movie?

7 Which song performed by Tom Jones featured in the movie *The Full Monty*?

8 Which soundtrack included the songs "Honey Bun" and "Happy Talk"?

9 Which trio sang six songs on the soundtrack for *Saturday Night Fever*?

10 Which Greek musician won an Oscar for his music in the movie *Chariots of Fire*?

Answers

Ennio Morricone

Frankie Avalon

Scott Joplin

Lionel Bart

The Bodyguard

The Exorcist

"You Can Leave Your Hat On"

South Pacific

The Bee Gees

Vangelis

Quiz 23
Question 2

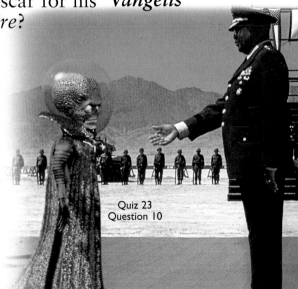

Quiz 23
Question 10

Quiz 25

Pick 'n' Mix

Questions	Answers
1 Which owner of a chocolate factory did Charlie Bucket meet on screen?	*Willy Wonka*
2 Which cartoon movie tells the story of a lost Russian princess?	**Anastasia**
3 Which American state shares its name with the first name of Dr. Jones?	*Indiana*
4 What is the name of Tarzan's female companion?	*Jane*
5 What is the name of Disney's flying elephant?	*Dumbo*
6 Which capital city did the Rugrats venture to in a 2000 movie?	*Paris*
7 What does the A stand for in the Steven Spielberg movie *A.I.*?	*Artificial*
8 What kind of animal is Maid Marian in Disney's cartoon version of *Robin Hood*?	*Fox*
9 What is the name of the young boy who is a close friend of Winnie the Pooh?	*Christopher Robin*
10 Which girl accompanied Peter Pan to Never Never Land?	*Wendy Darling*

Quiz 26
Question 2

Quiz 26
Question 3

Quiz 26

Popcorn – Kids

Questions	Answers
1 In which country is the Disney movie *Mulan* set?	*China*
2 What kind of creepy crawlies featured in the movie *Arachnophobia*?	*Spiders*
3 What kind of dinosaur is the monster featured in the 1998 movie *Godzilla*?	*Tyrannosaurus Rex*
4 Robbie Williams sang "We are the Champions" for which movie?	A Knight's Tale
5 How many of the seven dwarfs have a name beginning with S?	*Two – Sleepy and Sneezy*
6 In the 2002 animated movie what is the name of the stallion of the Cimarron?	Spirit
7 What is the name of the bird that Stuart Little rescues from the clutches of a falcon?	*Margalo*
8 Which 1997 cartoon film features the characters of Pain, Panic and Pegasus?	Hercules
9 To which islands do the Spy Kids venture in their second film outing?	*Islands of Lost Dreams*
10 What is the name of Fred Flintstone's best friend?	*Barney Rubble*

Quiz 25
Question 1

Quiz 25
Question 8

Quiz 27

At The Flicks – General

Questions	Answers
1 In which 1999 movie did Brendan Fraser play the all-action hero Rick O'Connell?	The Mummy
2 Which actor who starred in *The Champ* is the father of Angelina Jolie?	*Jon Voight*
3 Who played Oskar Schindler in the movie *Schindler's List*?	*Liam Neeson*
4 In which movie does Sean Connery play a submarine commander?	The Hunt for Red October
5 In which horror movie did Gregory Peck and Lee Remick play Damien's parents?	The Omen
6 When Dudley Moore played Dr. Watson, who played Sherlock Holmes?	*Peter Cook*
7 Which explorer was portrayed in the movie *1492: The Conquest of Paradise*?	*Christopher Columbus*
8 Whose 1987 autobiography is entitled *Also Known as Shirley*?	*Shelley Winters*
9 Which actor has played Batman, The Saint and Doc Holliday in movies?	*Val Kilmer*
10 In which city is the movie *Wall Street* set?	*New York*

Quiz 28
Question 7

Quiz 28
Question 4

Quiz 28

Preview – General

Questions	Answers
1 In which 1995 movie did Susan Sarandon wear a wimple?	Dead Man Walking
2 Which Icelandic pop star won a Best Actress award at the 2000 Cannes Film Festival?	*Bjork*
3 In the movie *Murder Most Foul*, which female sleuth solves the murder?	*Miss Marple*
4 In the movie *The Lavender Hill Mob*, gold bullion is made into models of what?	*Eiffel Tower*
5 Who played the title role in the 2001 movie *Miss Congeniality*?	*Sandra Bullock*
6 Which ex-husband of Barbra Streisand starred in *A Bridge Too Far*?	*Elliot Gould*
7 Mel Smith directed his friend Rowan Atkinson in which movie?	Bean
8 Which actor played Colonel Nathan R. Jessup in *A Few Good Men*?	*Jack Nicholson*
9 Which character was described as "The Barbarian" and "The Destroyer"?	*Conan*
10 Name Adolf Hitler's henchman in the movie *The Eagle Has Landed*.	*Heinrich Himmler*

Quiz 27
Question 1

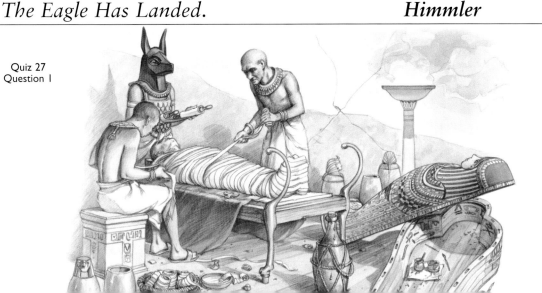

Quiz 29

Films In The War Years 1939–45

Questions	Answers
1 Which 1939 epic saw Olivia de Havilland playing Melanie Hamilton?	Gone with the Wind
2 Which movie masterpiece tells the story of newspaper tycoon Charles Foster Kane?	Citizen Kane
3 Which movie features "The Nutcracker Suite" and "The Sorcerer's Apprentice"?	Fantasia
4 Which scientist and Nobel Prize winner was played by Greer Garson in a 1943 movie?	*Marie Curie*
5 Dooley Wilson played Sam, the piano player, in which 1942 movie?	Casablanca
6 Which 1944 movie features a huge mansion called Thornfield Hall?	Jane Eyre
7 Which movie tells the tale of two old ladies who poison gentlemen callers at their home?	Arsenic and Old Lace
8 Where did Mr. Smith go to in a 1939 movie starring James Stewart?	*Washington*
9 Name the 1942 movie in which James Cagney plays a song and dance man.	Yankee Doodle Dandy
10 In which movie did John Wayne play the Ringo Kid?	Stagecoach

Quiz 30
Question 2

Quiz 30
Question 6

Quiz 30

Alfred Hitchcock

Questions	Answers
1 In which building did the murders take place in the movie *Psycho*?	*Bates Motel*
2 On which mountain does the climax of the movie *North by Northwest* take place?	*Mount Rushmore*
3 What is the title of the Hitchcock movie that featured the song "Que Sera Sera"?	**The Man who Knew too Much**
4 In which 1958 movie did James Stewart have a morbid fear of heights?	Vertigo
5 Which future princess starred in the movie *Dial M for Murder*?	*Grace Kelly*
6 In which movie does Melanie travel to Bodega Bay to meet a lawyer called Mitch?	**The Birds**
7 Name the actor who played Professor Michael Armstrong in *Torn Curtain*.	*Paul Newman*
8 Name the movie in which a wheelchair-bound photographer witnesses a murder.	**Rear Window**
9 In which movie did Cary Grant play a jewel thief called John Robie?	**To Catch a Thief**
10 What was Hitchcock's last movie as a director?	**Family Plot**

Quiz 29
Question 1

Quiz 29
Question 6

Quiz 31
The Name Game
Identify their movie star names

Questions	Answers
1 Caryn Johnson in *Ghost*	*Whoopi Goldberg*
2 Joyce Frankenberg in *Live and Let Die*	*Jane Seymour*
3 Allen Konigsberg in *The Purple Rose of Cairo*	*Woody Allen*
4 Jerome Silberman in *Blazing Saddles*	*Gene Wilder*
5 Camille Javal in *And God Created Woman*	*Brigitte Bardot*
6 Joseph Yule Jr. in *National Velvet*	*Mickey Rooney*
7 Taidje Khan Jr. in *The Magnificent Seven*	*Yul Brynner*
8 Anna Maria Italiano in *The Graduate*	*Anne Bancroft*
9 William Henry Pratt in *Frankenstein*	*Boris Karloff*
10 Bernard Schwartz in *The Vikings*	*Tony Curtis*

Quiz 32
Question 5

Quiz 32
Question 7

Quiz 32
Happy Birthday
Who am I?

Questions	Answers
1 Born 26 January 1925 in Cleveland, appeared in *The Towering Inferno*	*Paul Newman*
2 Born 10 February 1930 in Detroit, appeared in *The Towering Inferno*	*Robert Wagner*
3 Born 10 August 1960 in Malaga, appeared in *Interview with the Vampire*	*Antonio Banderas*
4 Born 31 August 1928 in Nebraska, appeared in *The Great Escape*	*James Coburn*
5 Born 22 February 1975 in Los Angeles, appeared in *Charlie's Angels*	*Drew Barrymore*
6 Born 25 February 1969 in Swansea, appeared in *Traffic*	*Catherine Zeta Jones*
7 Born 14 August 1968 in Cleveland, appeared in *Monster's Ball*	*Halle Berry*
8 Born 31 December 1937 in Port Talbot, appeared in *A Bridge Too Far*	*Anthony Hopkins*
9 Born 18 February 1954 in New Jersey, appeared in *Look Who's Talking*	*John Travolta*
10 Born 25 May 1939 in Burnley, appeared in *The Lord of the Rings*	*Ian McKellen*

Quiz 31
Question 1

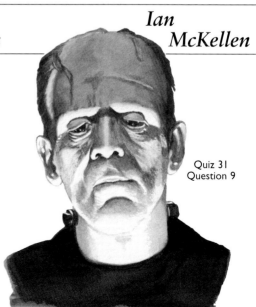

Quiz 31
Question 9

Quiz 33
Blockbusters

Questions	Answers
1 In which 2000 movie did Richard Harris play Emperor Marcus Aurelius?	**Gladiator**
2 Who played an oil driller called Harry Stamper in the movie *Armageddon*?	*Bruce Willis*
3 Which decade did Marty McFly travel back to in the 1985 movie *Back to the Future*?	*The 1950s*
4 *Planet of the Apes* (2001) is a remake of a movie starring which Hollywood legend?	*Charlton Heston*
5 What is the title of the 1997 movie that features a talking pug dog called Frank?	**Men in Black**
6 Neo, Trinity, Tank and Mouse are all characters in which 1999 movie?	**The Matrix**
7 What was the world's top box-office movie of the 1970s? Quiz 34 Question 1	**Star Wars**
8 In which 1993 movie is Dr. Richard Kimble wrongly accused of murdering his wife?	**The Fugitive**
9 Which 1996 movie saw Bill Paxton chasing tornadoes?	Twister
10 Which 1991 movie sequel is subtitled *Judgment Day*?	**Terminator II**

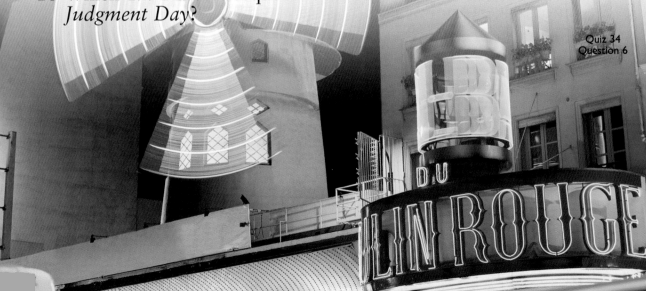

Quiz 34
Question 6

Quiz 34
Musical Medley

Questions	Answers
1 Which musical featured the song "Matchmaker, Matchmaker"?	Fiddler on the Roof
2 In which city is the 1972 musical *Cabaret* set? *Quiz 33 Question 9*	*Berlin*
3 What is the name of the rival gang of the Jets in *West Side Story*?	*The Sharks*
4 Which award-winning movie tells the story of a flower girl called Eliza Doolittle?	My Fair Lady
5 The song "Luck be a Lady" was heard in which musical starring Frank Sinatra?	Guys and Dolls
6 In which 2001 movie did Ewan McGregor play Christian?	Moulin Rouge
7 Deborah Kerr sang "Getting to Know You" to a group of children in which movie?	The King and I
8 What is the title of the musical that tells the story of the Pontabee siblings?	Seven Brides for Seven Brothers
9 In which movie did Jonathan Pryce play Madonna's husband?	Evita
10 Which 1979 movie was set at the New York School of Performing Arts?	Fame

Quiz 33
Question 1

Quiz 35

Steven Spielberg

Questions	Answers
1 What was the tagline for *Close Encounters of the Third Kind?*	"We are not alone"
2 Which 1993 blockbuster co-starred Laura Dern, Jeff Goldblum and Sam Neill?	Jurassic Park
3 Which movie earned Spielberg his first Oscar for Best Director?	Schindler's List
4 In which country are the battle scenes of *Saving Private Ryan* set?	France
5 What is the name of the boat skippered by Captain Quint in the movie *Jaws?*	*The Orca*
6 What is the title of Spielberg's 1991 adaptation of the story of Peter Pan?	Hook
7 Name the leading lady in the Spielberg movie *Indiana Jones and the Temple of Doom.*	*Kate Capshaw*
8 Which 2002 movie starring Tom Cruise is set in the year 2054?	Minority Report
9 In which movie does a gang of children search for the treasure of "One Eyed" Willy?	The Goonies
10 In what decade was Spielberg born?	*1940s – born in 1946*

Quiz 36
Question 2

Quiz 36
Question 10

Quiz 36
Animated Antics

Questions	Answers
1 Jafar is the name of the villain in which 1992 Disney movie?	**Aladdin**
2 Name the movie in which Gene Kelly dances with Jerry from the *Tom and Jerry* cartoons.	**Anchors Aweigh**
3 Which actor links *The Flintstones*, *Ghostbusters* and *Honey I Shrunk the Kids*?	*Rick Moranis*
4 In which animation does the character of Richard Tyler meet Long John Silver?	**The Pagemaster**
5 Uncle Remus recounts the tales of Brer Rabbit and Brer Fox in which 1946 movie?	**Song of the South**
6 Which 1999 cartoon movie is subtitled *Bigger, Longer and Uncut*?	**South Park**
7 In 2002 the first Oscar for Best Animation went to which movie?	**Shrek**
8 Who provided the voice of Mickey Mouse in his cartoon debut?	*Walt Disney*
9 J. Worthington Foulfellow, Stromboli and Figaro are all characters in which movie?	**Pinocchio**
10 Which movie tells the story of a Hawaiian girl who adopts a dog that is disguised as an alien?	**Lilo and Stitch**

Quiz 35
Question 6

Quiz 35
Question 9

Quiz 37

Dressing Room – General

Questions	Answers
1 In which movie did Tom Hanks play a boy trapped in a 32-year-old man's body?	**Big**
2 In the title of a 1999 movie, a dragon is hiding and what animal is crouching?	*Tiger*
3 When Olivia de Havilland played Maid Marian, who played *Robin Hood*?	*Errol Flynn*
4 Who played Rita in *Educating Rita*?	*Julie Walters*
5 Which movie star is the daughter of director John Huston?	*Angelica Huston*
6 In which 1990 movie did Julia Roberts and Kiefer Sutherland play medical students?	**Flatliners**
7 In which 1968 movie did Sally Anne Howes play Truly Scrumptious?	**Chitty Chitty Bang Bang**
8 In which 1997 movie did Gaz, Gerald, Guy and Dave shed their clothes?	**The Full Monty**
9 Which Scottish comedian played an auctioneer in *Indecent Proposal*?	*Billy Connolly*
10 In a 1993 version of *The Three Musketeers* who played D'Artagnan?	*Chris O'Donnell*

Quiz 38
Question 10

Quiz 38
Question 6

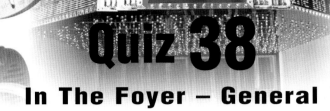

Questions	Answers
1 What is the name of the arch enemy of Austin Powers?	*Dr. Evil*
2 Which singer did Val Kilmer play in the 1991 movie *The Doors*?	*Jim Morrison*
3 Which movie starring Whoopi Goldberg is also the title of a Rolling Stones hit record?	**Jumping Jack Flash**
4 Who did Rosie O'Donnell play in the 1994 movie *The Flintstones*?	*Betty Rubble*
5 In which 1997 movie did Mel Gibson play a paranoid character called Jerry Fletcher?	**Conspiracy Theory**
6 Which 1950 musical told the story of the wild west heroine Annie Oakley?	**Annie Get Your Gun**
7 *Jason Takes Manhattan* is the sub-title of the 8th movie in which series of horror flicks?	**Friday the 13th**
8 In which 1993 movie does Kevin Kline impersonate the President of the U.S.A.?	**Dave**
9 In which movie does a weatherman have to live the same day over and over again?	**Groundhog Day**
10 Which 1998 movie saw Wesley Snipes vanquishing vampires?	**Blade**

Quiz 37
Question 2

Quiz 39
Showbiz Animals

Questions	Answers
1 In which 1988 movie did James Belushi play a narcotics cop who teamed up with a dog?	K-9
2 What was the title of the 1943 movie that saw the debut of Lassie?	Lassie Come Home
3 Which screen cowboy of yesteryear rode a horse called "Topper"?	*Hopalong Cassidy*
4 What breed of dog is Beethoven in the 1992 movie?	*St. Bernard*
5 Which sequel features Lennie the weasel, Joey the raccoon and Archie the bear?	Dr Doolittle II
6 What was the name of Roy Rogers' dog?	*Bullet*
7 Fiver and Hazel are the names of rabbits in which movie?	Watership Down
8 In the 1956 movie version of *Moby Dick* who played the role of Captain Ahab?	*Gregory Peck*
9 In which 1971 Disney movie did a duck lay eggs with solid gold yolks?	Million Dollar Duck
10 In the 1972 movie *Ben*, is Ben a cat, a rat or a horse?	*Rat*

Quiz 40
Question 3

Quiz 40
Question 7

Quiz 40
Question 8

Quiz 40
Sports On Film

Questions	Answers
1 In the 1974 movie *The Mean Machine*, who played a former pro-footballer Paul Crewe?	*Burt Reynolds*
2 Which *Z Cars* actor won an Oscar for Best Screenplay for the movie *Chariots of Fire*?	*Colin Welland*
3 What sport features in the 1993 movie *The Sandlot*?	*Baseball*
4 The movie *When We Were Kings* chronicles Muhammad Ali's fight with which boxer?	*George Foreman*
5 What is the title of the 1986 movie in which Paul Newman plays a pool hustler?	**The Color of Money**
6 Who kept goal for the allied team in *Escape to Victory*?	*Sylvester Stallone*
7 Who played golf pro Roy McAvoy in the 1996 movie *Tin Cup*?	*Kevin Costner*
8 What sport is featured in *Pharlap*, *Champions* and *The Shamrock Handicap*?	*Horseracing*
9 What number appears on the side of Herbie, the VW Beetle racing car in *The Love Bug*?	*53*
10 Who played Rod Tidwell, wide receiver for the Arizona Cardinals, in *Jerry Maguire*?	*Cuba Gooding Jr.*

Quiz 39
Question 10

Quiz 39
Question 4

Quiz 41

Crocodile Dundee

Questions	Answers
1 What is Crocodile Dundee's first name?	*Mick*
2 To which U.S. city does Crocodile Dundee travel in the third movie of the series?	*Los Angeles*
3 In which year was the first *Crocodile Dundee* movie made?	*1986*
4 Who plays the role of Sue Charlton in the *Crocodile Dundee* movies?	*Linda Kozlowski*
5 What is the first name of Dundee's Australian sidekick played by John Meillon?	*Wally*
6 Which group had a hit with the song from *Crocodile Dundee* entitled "Live it Up"?	*Mental as Anything*
7 What is the name of Crocodile Dundee's hometown in Australia?	*Walkabout Creek*
8 What is the name of Sue and Dundee's nine-year-old son in the third movie?	*Mikey*
9 To which U.S. city did Dundee travel with Sue Charlton in the first movie?	*New York*
10 What does Crocodile Dundee call women?	*Sheilas*

Quiz 42
Question 6

Questions	Answers
1 Who had a hit with the theme song from the original *Ghostbusters* movie?	*Robert Parker Jr.*
2 In which 1982 movie is a family's youngest daughter kidnapped by ghosts?	Poltergeist
3 Who played Molly in the movie *Ghost*?	*Demi Moore*
4 In which ghost story does Nicole Kidman star as the mother of two young children?	The Others
5 Who played the title role in *Beetlejuice*?	*Michael Keaton*
6 In which 1999 movie did Haley Joel Osment say, "I see dead people"?	The Sixth Sense
7 In which ghost story were Harrison Ford and Michelle Pfeiffer haunted?	What Lies Beneath
8 Who plays Dr. Raymond Stantz in *Ghostbusters*?	*Dan Aykroyd*
9 Which children's character is described as "The Friendly Ghost"?	*Casper*
10 In which movie does Margaret Rutherford play Madame Arcati?	Blithe Spirit

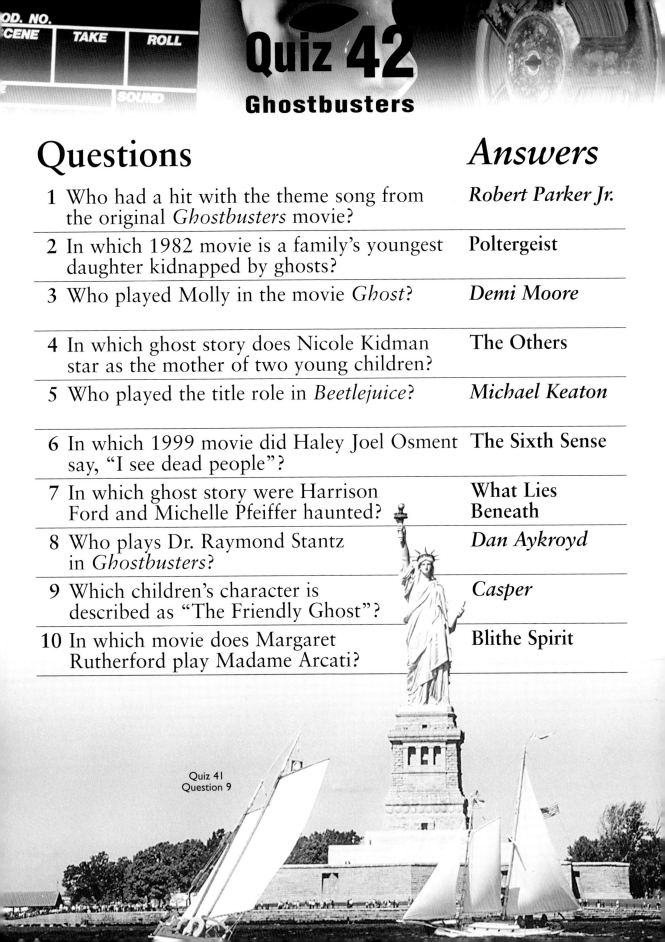

Quiz 41
Question 9

Quiz 43

Front Row Seats

Questions	Answers
1 Who played Chief Brody in the movie *Jaws*?	*Roy Scheider*
2 Which star of *Bedtime for Bonzo* went on to become a world leader?	*Ronald Reagan*
3 Who plays the title role in the 2002 movie *The Bourne Identity*?	*Matt Damon*
4 Which Scottish actor voiced a dragon called Draco in the movie *Dragonheart*?	*Sean Connery*
5 Who died aged 36 shortly after making the movie *The Misfits*?	*Marilyn Monroe*
6 Which 2001 movie includes the surname of England's 2002 Football World Cup captain?	**Bend it Like Beckham**
7 For which comedy western did Lee Marvin win an Oscar for playing twin brothers?	**Cat Ballou**
8 Which footballer connects the movies *Snatch*, *Swordfish* and *Gone in 60 Seconds*?	*Vinnie Jones*
9 Which animator created Wallace and Gromit?	*Nick Park*
10 What is the title of the 1997 movie in which John Travolta plays an angel?	**Michael**

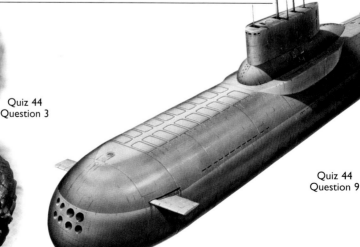

Quiz 44
Question 3

Quiz 44
Question 9

Quiz 44

Questions	Answers
1 In which movie does Kevin Bacon discover the secret of invisibility?	Hollow Man
2 What kind of shop was owned by Hugh Grant in *Notting Hill*?	*A bookshop*
3 In which country was Billy Hayes imprisoned in *Midnight Express*?	*Turkey*
4 In what movie, an update of *Cyrano de Bergerac*, did Steve Martin play a firefighter?	Roxanne
5 Who did Buster Crabbe play on movie when he was battling against Ming the Merciless?	Flash Gordon
6 Who plays a female ape called Ari in the 2001 movie *Planet of the Apes*?	*Helena Bonham Carter*
7 Who starred in the movie *Clockwise* as a headmaster called Mr. Stimpson?	*John Cleese*
8 Who played the police detective Officer Nordberg in *Naked Gun*?	*O.J. Simpson*
9 What connects *Crimson Tide, The Enemy Below* and *The Hunt for Red October*?	*Submarines*
10 In which movie did James Dean play the role of Jim Stark?	Rebel Without A Cause

Some Like It Hot

Questions	Answers
1 Which knighted actor played God in the comedy movie *Time Bandits*?	*Sir Ralph Richardson*
2 What was the first *Carry On* movie?	Carry On Sergeant
3 According to the title of a 1977 movie, what is the name of Dracula's dog?	Zoltan
4 The climax of *The Third Man* takes place in the sewers of which capital city?	*Vienna*
5 In *When Harry Met Sally*, what is Harry's last name?	*Burns*
6 Who did Charlton Heston portray in *The Agony and the Ecstasy*?	*Michelangelo*
7 Which 1981 Oscar-winning movie chronicles the life story of John Reed?	**Reds**
8 Who wore a cantilevered bra, specially designed for her in *The Outlaw*?	*Jane Russell*
9 Which Disney character married Faline?	Bambi
10 Who wrote the play *Still Life* on which the classic love story *Brief Encounter* is based?	*Sir Noel Coward*

Quiz 46
Question 10

Quiz 46

True Grit

Questions	Answers
1 The 1999 movie, *10 Things I Hate About You*, was based on which Shakespeare play?	The Taming of The Shrew
2 Which 1996 movie is based on the life of pianist David Helfgott?	Shine
3 What was Edith Head listed as in over 300 movies from the 1930s to the 1980s?	*Costume designer*
4 Which movie starring Jane Fonda was based on a comic strip by Jean Claude Forest?	Barbarella
5 Who played the leading lady alongside Bob Hope and Bing Crosby in the road movies?	*Dorothy Lamour*
6 Who played Inspector Clouseau in the 1968 movie entitled *Inspector Clouseau*?	*Alan Arkin*
7 The movie *The Music Lovers* was based on the life of which classical composer?	*Tchaikovsky*
8 What was the title of the first sound movie that featured Mickey Mouse?	Steamboat Willie
9 Which movie with Richard Burton was the first to be filmed in cinemascope?	The Robe
10 In which 1995 movie did Sophie Marceau play Princess Isabelle?	Braveheart

Quiz 45
Question 9

Quiz 47
Pick 'n' Mix

Questions	Answers
1 What is the name of the tomb raider played on screen by Angelina Jolie?	*Lara Croft*
2 Which *Friends* actress is married to the movie star David Arquette?	*Courtney Cox*
3 Which man of steel is vulnerable when exposed to kryptonite?	*Superman*
4 In the movie *Grease,* does Danny fall in love with Sindy, Sandy or Mandy?	*Sandy*
5 Which sport features in the movie *The Bad News Bears*?	*Baseball*
6 What kind of toy bird is Wheezy in *Toy Story II*?	*Penguin*
7 Who gains his strength from eating spinach?	*Popeye*
8 Which movie is introduced with the words, "A long time ago in a galaxy far, far away"?	**Star Wars**
9 In which country was Arnold Schwarzenegger born?	*Austria*
10 In which movie did Lindsay Lohan play twin sisters?	**The Parent Trap**

Quiz 48
Question 7

Quiz 48
Popcorn

Questions	Answers
1 In which Disney movie does a spaniel fall in love with a mongrel?	**Lady and the Tramp**
2 The wrestler "The Rock" played which king in *The Mummy Returns*?	*The Scorpion King*
3 What type of creatures are Sam, Merry and Pippin in *The Lord of the Rings*?	*Hobbits*
4 What is the name of the evil lord in the movie *Shrek*?	*Lord Farquaad*
5 Is the hero of the movie *Chicken Run* called Ricky, Stocky or Rocky?	*Rocky*
6 What part of the body is the scarecrow searching for in *The Wizard of Oz*?	*The brain*
7 In which movie did an alien phone home with the help of Elliot?	E.T.
8 In which movie did Robin Williams dress up as a nanny?	**Mrs. Doubtfire**
9 Which American wrestler appeared in the movies *Rocky III* and *Muppets From Space*?	*Hulk Hogan*
10 In which animated movie does a captain fall in love with an American Indian princess?	**Pocahontas**

Quiz 47
Question 6

Quiz 47
Question 5

Questions	Answers
1 Who won consecutive Best Actor Oscars in the 1990s?	*Tom Hanks*
2 Which actress played Karen Silkwood, Lindy Chamberlain and Sarah Woodrough?	*Meryl Streep*
3 Which star of the TV sitcom *Cheers* played Dad in *Getting Even With Dad*?	*Ted Danson*
4 Which movie star of yesteryear was nicknamed "The Sweater Girl"?	*Lana Turner*
5 Who played Bridget Jones on screen?	*Renee Zellwegger*
6 Who was nominated for the Best Actor Oscar in 1995 for *Witness*?	*Harrison Ford*
7 Which actor played the detective Eddie Valiant in *Who Framed Roger Rabbit*?	*Bob Hoskins*
8 Who made a tearful Oscar acceptance speech for her role in *Shakespeare in Love*?	*Gwyneth Paltrow*
9 Which mythical creature featured in the movie *Splash!*?	*Mermaid*
10 Which duo sang "Trail of the Lonesome Pine" in *Way Out West*?	*Laurel and Hardy*

Quiz 50
Question 8

Quiz 50
Question 1

Quiz 50

Keep It In The Family

Questions	Answers
1 Which movie featured a pair of unlikely brothers called Julius and Vincent Benedict?	Twins
2 What is the family connection between *Easy Rider*, *Klute* and *Twelve Angry Men*?	*The Fonda family*
3 In which heist movie did Steve McQueen star with his then wife Ali McGraw?	The Getaway
4 Which father of two movie actor sons starred in *Apocalypse Now*?	*Martin Sheen*
5 Name the actress mother of Mia Farrow, who starred in several *Tarzan* movies as Jane.	*Maureen O'Sullivan*
6 Which movie legend married Frank Sinatra, Mickey Rooney and Artie Shaw?	*Ava Gardner*
7 Name Warren Beatty's sister who starred in *Terms of Endearment*.	*Shirley MacLaine*
8 In which movie did Elizabeth Taylor first star with Richard Burton?	Cleopatra
9 Which of the Baldwin brothers married Kim Basinger?	*Alec Baldwin*
10 Who is the movie star mother of Carrie Fisher?	*Debbie Reynolds*

Quiz 49
Question 9

Quiz 49
Question 8

Quiz 51
Movie Quotes

Questions	Answers
1 Which 1995 movie was introduced by, "Five criminals, one line-up, no coincidence"?	The Usual Suspects
2 Which character was Clint Eastwood playing when he said, "Go ahead, make my day"?	*Harry Callahan*
3 Which movie ended with the words, "Tomorrow is another day"?	Gone with the Wind
4 Which movie contains the following line, "It's dark and we're wearing sunglasses"?	The Blues Brothers
5 Which character is associated with the catchphrase, "To infinity and beyond"?	*Buzz Lightyear*
6 In which movie did Arnold Schwarzenegger first utter the line, "I'll be back"?	Terminator
7 Which actor on screen said, "Do you think we used enough dynamite there Butch?"	*Robert Redford as Butch Cassidy*
8 In which movie did Michael Douglas say, "Greed for lack of a better word is good"?	Wall Street
9 Which movie includes the line, "If you played it for her you can play it for me"?	Casablanca
10 In the 1949 movie *White Heat*, who said, "Made it ma! Top of the world!"?	*James Cagney*

Quiz 52
Question 9

Quiz 52
Question 8

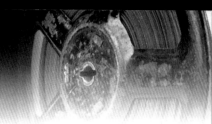

Quiz 52
Movie Lingo

Questions	Answers
1 What is added to a movie by a foley artist?	*Sound effects*
2 What genre of movies are known as "horse operas" in the movie business?	*Westerns*
3 On a movie set, what job is done by the gaffer?	*Chief electrician*
4 What was the name given to a plank of wood actors stood on to make them appear taller?	*Pancake*
5 On a movie set what name is given to a microphone attached to a long pole?	*Boom microphone*
6 Why does Ian Smithee sometimes appear at the end of movie credits?	*A director's alias*
7 What is arranged by a choreographer?	*Dance sequence*
8 What is the name of the small truck that carries the camera and the camera operater?	*Dolly*
9 What is the name of the board that is placed in front of camera before each shot?	*Clapperboard*
10 What name is given to a cast member used to take the place of an actor for a specific scene?	*Body double*

Quiz 51
Question 4

Quiz 53

Make The Connection
Name the movie stars who link each group of three movies

Questions

1 *One Fine Day, Dangerous Liaisons* and *Batman Returns?*

2 *Superman III, Harlem Nights* and *Stir Crazy?*

3 *Nine Months, The Lost World: Jurassic Park* and *Hannibal?* *Quiz 54 Question 8*

4 *The Mexican, Twelve Monkeys* and *Meet Joe Black?*

5 *Breakfast at Tiffany's, My Fair Lady* and *Roman Holiday?*

6 *The Sound of Music, International Velvet* and *Waterloo?*

7 *Enemy of the State, The Legend of Bagger Vance* and *Independence Day?*

8 *Fletch, The Three Amigos* and *Spies Like Us?*

9 *The Defiant Ones, Guess Who's Coming to Dinner* and *To Sir with Love?*

10 *Overboard, The First Wives Club* and *Private Benjamin?*

Answers

Michelle Pfeiffer

Richard Pryor

Julianne Moore

Brad Pitt

Audrey Hepburn

Christopher Plummer

Will Smith

Chevy Chase

Sidney Poitier

Goldie Hawn

Quiz 54 Question 3

Quiz 54

The Oscars

Name the Best Actor/Actress Oscar winners in the movies below

Questions	Answers
1 Best Actress – *As Good as it Gets*	Helen Hunt
2 Best Actor – *The Scent of a Woman*	Al Pacino
3 Best Actor – *Kramer versus Kramer*	Dustin Hoffman
4 Best Actress – *The Accused*	Jodie Foster
5 Best Actor – *Leaving Las Vegas*	Nicholas Cage
6 Best Actress – *Annie Hall*	Diane Keaton
7 Best Actor – *To Kill a Mockingbird*	Gregory Peck
8 Best Actress – *The Piano*	Holly Hunter
9 Best Actress – *Driving Miss Daisy*	Jessica Tandy
10 Best Actor – *Reversal of Fortune*	Jeremy Irons

Quiz 53
Question 5

Quiz 53
Question 7

Quiz 55
There Goes That Song Again

Questions	Answers
1 What did the nuns change the title of "My Guy" to in *Sister Act*?	*"My God"*
2 Which musical features the song, "Surrey with the Fringe on Top"?	Oklahoma
3 Which song featured in the movies *Unchained* and *Ghost*?	*"Unchained Melody"*
4 The song "Big Spender" features in which movie and stage show?	Sweet Charity
5 Which character sang "As Long as he Needs Me" in the musical *Oliver*?	*Nancy*
6 Which Buddy Holly hit is also the title of a 1973 movie starring David Essex?	*"That'll be the Day"*
7 In which movie was Lee Marvin "born under a wandrin' star"?	Paint Your Wagon
8 For which movie did Wet Wet Wet record the song "Love is all Around"?	Four Weddings and a Funeral
9 Which song connects *The Bodyguard* and *The Best Little Whorehouse in Texas*?	*"I Will Always Love You"*
10 "Up Where We Belong" is a song from which movie starring Richard Gere?	An Officer and a Gentleman

Quiz 56
Question 1

Questions	Answers
1 What was The Beatles first movie?	A Hard Day's Night
2 What land did The Beatles venture into in the animated movie *Yellow Submarine*?	*Pepperland*
3 Name Ringo Starr's actress wife who starred in *The Spy Who Loved Me*.	*Barbara Bach*
4 Which actor, famous for being Alf Garnett, played Abdul in *Help*?	*Warren Mitchell*
5 Which movie starring Paul McCartney featured the song "No More Lonely Nights"?	Give my Regards to Broad Street
6 What is the name of the movie production company established by George Harrison?	*Handmade Films*
7 Are the Meanies in the movie *Yellow Submarine*, red, blue, yellow or green?	*Blue*
8 Which movie featuring The Beatles was also the name of one of their final studio album?	Let it Be
9 Which Bond theme was written and performed by Paul McCartney?	*"Live and Let Die"*
10 Which 1967 black comedy set during World War II co-starred John Lennon?	How I Won the War

Quiz 55
Question 10

Quiz 57
Choc Ices

Questions	Answers
1 Which movie features the characters Agent J and Agent K?	Men in Black
2 In which 2000 comedy did Jonathan Lipnicki play a young bloodsucker?	The Little Vampire
3 Which of the seven dwarfs wears glasses?	*Doc*
4 Which reptile is Indiana Jones terrified of?	*Snakes*
5 What kind of animals are Scar and Simba?	*Lions*
6 Which Disney movie features the characters of Thomas O'Malley and Duchess?	The Aristocats
7 In which movie do two dogs and a cat attempt to find their way home?	Homeward Bound
8 *The Adventure Home* and *The Rescue* are both sequels to which movie about a whale?	Free Willy
9 The song "Walking in the Air" is heard in which animated movie?	The Snowman
10 In which movie did Cameron Diaz play the role of Mary?	There's Something About Mary

Quiz 58
Question 2

Quiz 58
Question 9

Quiz 58
Question 4

Quiz 58

Hot Dogs

Questions	Answers
1 The character of Milo Thatch appears in which Disney movie about a lost empire?	Atlantis
2 On what type of transport did E.T. and Elliot escape from government officials?	*Bicycles*
3 What letter of the alphabet is the code name for James Bond's boss?	M
4 In which movie did King Louie sing "I Wanna be like You"?	The Jungle Book
5 On screen what kind of animals are Skip, Benji and Rin Tin Tin?	*Dogs*
6 In which direction does the cartoon mouse Fievel travel in a 1991 movie?	*West*
7 What is the name of the wood where Winnie the Pooh lives?	*Hundred Acre Wood*
8 Which series of movies features the characters of Bilbo Baggins and Sauron?	The Lord of the Rings
9 Which 1999 teen comedy is also the title of a 2000 hit for Madonna?	American Pie
10 In which war is *Pearl Harbor* set?	*World War II*

Quiz 57
Question 9

Quiz 57
Question 8

Quiz 57
Question 4

Stage Door Anagrams

Unravel the anagrams to give the titles of ten popular movies

Questions	Answers
1 GO NUN GUYS	Young Guns
2 GIST THEN	The Sting
3 SCARE LOU	Carousel
4 VINE FOR GUN	Unforgiven
5 SHEENS HIS TEXT	The Sixth Sense
6 I NIT CAT	Titanic
7 BEN CLAM KIN	Men in Black
8 NAAN RIM	Rain Man
9 TON TAP	Patton
10 KEMON ROAR	Moonraker

Quiz 60
Question 1

Quiz 60

Preview Anagrams

Unravel the anagrams to give the titles of ten popular movies

Questions	Answers
1 HAD GIN	Gandhi
2 STUMP FORGER	Forrest Gump
3 BRED THIS	The Birds
4 I LOVER	Oliver
5 REV A BERTHA	Braveheart
6 CEDED POLO HUT	The Odd Couple
7 TOOL PAN	Platoon
8 SUIT WHEY SEED	Eyes Wide Shut
9 MUM BURN BED DAD	Dumb and Dumber
10 MEAN DRIPS	Spiderman

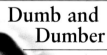

Quiz 59
Question 10

Quiz 59
Question 6

Quiz 59
Question 3

Questions	Answers
1 Who battled against aliens in *Independence Day* and against dinosaurs in *Jurassic Park*?	*Jeff Goldblum*
2 Which singer won an Oscar for her role in *Moonstruck*?	*Cher*
3 Which bridge sees the climax of the James Bond movie *A View to a Kill*?	*Golden Gate Bridge*
4 Which movie tells the story of Jim Garrison's investigation into a 1963 assassination?	**JFK**
5 What was Marilyn Monroe's sweet first name in *Some Like It Hot*?	*Sugar*
6 What was the first movie to feature the character of Indiana Jones?	**Raiders of the Lost Ark**
7 Which Hollywood legend was the subject of the 1983 movie *Mommie Dearest*?	*Joan Crawford*
8 Which actor was born Archibald Leach?	*Cary Grant*
9 In which 1991 movie does Billy Crystal embark on a cattle-driving holiday?	**City Slickers**
10 In which 1976 movie did Jodie Foster play a gangster's moll?	**Bugsy Malone**

Quiz 62
Question 10

Quiz 62

In The Back Row

Questions	Answers
1 Who provided the voice of Mikey in *Look Who's Talking*?	*Bruce Willis*
2 Which actress played Honey Rider in *Dr. No*?	*Ursula Andress*
3 *Gone with the Wind* was set during which war?	*The American Civil War*
4 In which Oscar-winning epic did Oliver Reed make his screen farewell?	Gladiator
5 Which 2002 psychological thriller co-stars Al Pacino and Robin Williams?	Insomnia
6 Who played King Arthur in *Monty Python and the Holy Grail*?	*Graham Chapman*
7 What is the title of the sequel to *Bill and Ted's Excellent Adventure*?	**Bill and Ted's Bogus Journey**
8 Alphabetically, who is the last Marx brother?	*Zeppo*
9 In which comedy does Jim Carrey play a state trooper with a split personality?	**Me, Myself and Irene**
10 Which infamous brothers were played by Gary and Martin Kemp in a 1990 movie?	*The Krays*

Quiz 61
Question 6

Quiz 63

Hot Dogs

Unravel the anagrams to give the names of Disney movies and Disney characters

Questions	Answers
1 DOOR IN HOB	Robin Hood
2 NAZ RAT	Tarzan
3 SEE MUCKY MOI	*Mickey Mouse*
4 PERM HUT	*Thumper*
5 DAN LAID	Aladdin
6 MI GLOW	*Mowgli*
7 PIN MOP SPRAY	Mary Poppins
8 NEW RING LADDY	*Wendy Darling*
9 A FAST IAN	Fantasia
10 RED LACE NIL	Cinderella

Quiz 64
Question 9

Quiz 64
Question 10

Quiz 64

Popcorn

Unravel the anagrams to give the names of Disney movies and Disney characters

Questions	Answers
1 MA BIB	**Bambi**
2 PANT PEER	**Peter Pan**
3 LACK DUD NOD	*Donald Duck*
4 PACK IN A HOOT	*Captain Hook*
5 HE NOT NGIKIL	The Lion King
6 FAB LUSH	*Bashful*
7 SHE CRUEL	Hercules
8 HERES HANK	*Shere Khan*
9 I GLUES FAB	A Bug's Life
10 NICE N STORMS	Monsters Inc.

Quiz 63
Question 1

Quiz 65
John Wayne

Questions	Answers
1 Despite his tough guy image, what was Wayne's real name?	*Marion Morrison*
2 Which 1968 movie, directed by and starring Wayne, was about the Vietnam War?	**The Green Berets**
3 Who did he portray in *The Alamo*?	*Davy Crockett*
4 What was Joanne Dru wearing according to the title of a 1949 Wayne movie?	*A yellow ribbon*
5 For which movie did he win his only Best Actor Oscar?	**True Grit**
6 In which 1965 movie was Wayne reunited with his brothers at a funeral?	**The Sons of Katie Elder**
7 Which 1976 movie saw Wayne's last screen appearance as gunslinger J.B. Books?	**The Shootist**
8 Which ancient leader did he play in the 1953 movie *The Conqueror*?	*Genghis Khan*
9 In which 1952 movie, set in Ireland, did he co-star with Maureen O'Hara?	**The Quiet Man**
10 How did Wayne acquire his nickname, "The Duke"?	*From his pet dog, Duke*

Quiz 66
Question 1

Quiz 66
Question 9

Quiz 66
Titanic Trivia

Questions	Answers
1 What is the first name of the character played by Kate Winslet in *Titanic*?	*Rose*
2 Who directed the 1997 movie *Titanic*?	*James Cameron*
3 Who played the captain of the *Titanic* in the movie?	*Bernard Hill*
4 What was the title of Celine Dion's hit single from the movie *Titanic*?	*"My Heart Will Go On"*
5 In what year was the movie *Titanic* mostly set?	*1912*
6 What is the first name of the character played by Leonardo DiCaprio?	*Jack*
7 Who played Cal Hockley, Kate Winslet's fiancée in the movie?	*Billy Zane*
8 How many Oscar nominations did *Titanic* receive?	*14 nominations, winning 11*
9 Which Oscar-winning actress played the role of Molly Brown?	*Kathy Bates*
10 Who plays Brock Lovett, the salvage operator, in the 1997 movie?	*Bill Paxton*

Quiz 65
Question 8

Quiz 65
Question 5

Quiz 67
Movie Flops

Questions	Answers
1 Which 1986 musical was a huge box-office flop for David Bowie and Patsy Kensit?	**Absolute Beginners**
2 Whose adventures were a 1989 box-office flop for director Terry Gilliam?	*Baron Munchausen*
3 Kevin Costner played the mariner in which expensive movie flop?	**Waterworld**
4 Which 1987 comedy flop set in Morocco starred Dustin Hoffman and Warren Beatty?	**Ishtar**
5 In which 1998 box-office flop was Harrison Ford marooned on a desert island?	**Six Days and Seven Nights**
6 Which 1995 movie panned by the critics saw Geena Davis playing a female pirate?	**Cutthroat Island**
7 What was the name of the cat burglar played by Bruce Willis in the 1991 movie flop?	*Hudson Hawk*
8 Which World War II movie starring John Belushi was a rare flop for Steven Spielberg?	**1941**
9 Which 1980 western starring Kris Kristofferson was a financial disaster?	**Heaven's Gate**
10 About which movie was it said, "It would have been cheaper to lower the Atlantic"?	**Raise the Titanic**

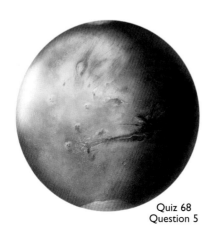

Quiz 68
Question 5

Quiz 68
Question 2

Questions	Answers
1 In which 1994 *Star Trek* movie did Captain Kirk join forces with Captain Picard?	**Star Trek: Generations**
2 Citizens were terminated at the age of 30 in which futuristic 1976 sci-fi movie?	**Logan's Run**
3 What is the four-letter name of Marty McFly's foe in *Back to the Future*?	*Biff*
4 Which 1984 movie starring Sting is set in the year 10991 on the desert planet of Arakis?	**Dune**
5 Which planet did Arnold Schwarzenegger travel to in *Total Recall*?	*Mars*
6 What make of car does Dr. Brown employ as a time machine in *Back to the Future*?	*De Lorean*
7 *The Road Warrior* and *Beyond Thunderdome* were sequels to which movie?	**Mad Max**
8 In which movie was an L.A. cop released from suspended animation in the year 2032?	**Demolition Man**
9 James Caan is the star player of a violent sport of the future in which 1975 movie?	**Rollerball**
10 Kurt Russell attempts to rescue the U.S. president from a prison in which movie?	**Escape from New York**

Quiz 67
Question 1

Quiz 67
Question 10

Quiz 69
Pick 'n' Mix

Questions	Answers
1 What is the name of the black- and red-faced villain in *Star Wars: The Phantom Menace*?	*Darth Maul*
2 What plant is Count Dracula repelled by?	*Garlic*
3 In which Christmas movie does Dudley Moore play an elf?	**Santa Claus: The Movie**
4 Which series of books by J.K. Rowling have been turned into blockbuster movies?	Harry Potter
5 In a fairytale animated by Disney studios, who falls in love with Prince Charming?	*Cinderella*
6 Who played Ethan Hunt in the movie *Mission Impossible*?	*Tom Cruise*
7 Which movie star and rap artist played Muhammad Ali in the 2001 movie *Ali*?	*Will Smith*
8 Which actor links the roles of Indiana Jones, Han Solo and Dr. Kimble?	*Harrison Ford*
9 Which Disney animation is based on the novel *Treasure Island*?	Treasure Planet
10 What is Jim Carrey's occupation in the movie *Liar, Liar*?	*Lawyer*

Quiz 70
Question 3

Quiz 70
Question 6

Quiz 70
Popcorn

Questions	Answers
1 What is the name of the Emperor who is the arch enemy of Buzz Lightyear?	*Emperor Zurg*
2 Who recorded the song "I Don't Want to Miss a Thing" for *Armageddon*?	*Aerosmith*
3 Who wrote the novel on which the musical *Oliver* was based?	*Charles Dickens*
4 Which star of the sitcom *Friends* appears in *Analyze This*?	*Lisa Kudrow*
5 Who plays the title role in the 2002 movie *Pluto Nash*?	*Eddie Murphy*
6 Who does Robin Williams provide the voice for in Disney's *Aladdin*?	*The Genie*
7 Which foe of Batman was played on screen by Jack Nicholson?	*The Joker*
8 In which series of sci-fi thrillers does Sigourney Weaver play Ellen Ripley?	**Alien**
9 Which American pop sensation made her big screen debut in the movie *Crossroads*?	*Britney Spears*
10 What sort of creature is Legolas in *The Lord of the Rings* trilogy?	*Elf*

Quiz 69
Question 2

Quiz 69
Question 4

Quiz 71
Creature Comforts

Questions	Answers
1 What kind of animal is Pegasus in Disney's *Hercules*?	*Horse*
2 What kind of animal is Pummba in *The Lion King*?	*Warthog*
3 What kind of animal is Andre in the movie of the same name?	*Sea lion*
4 What kind of birds were flying home in the movie *Fly Away Home*?	*Geese*
5 What kind of animal is Colonel Hathi in *The Jungle Book*?	*Elephant*
6 What kind of animal is Wol in the *Winnie the Pooh* movies?	*Owl*
7 What kind of family pet is Cleo in *Pinocchio*?	*Goldfish*
8 What kind of animal is Orion in *Men in Black*?	*Cat*
9 What kind of animal is Sir Hiss in Disney's *Robin Hood*?	*Snake*
10 What kind of animal is Timothy in *Dumbo*?	*Mouse*

Quiz 72
Question 10

Quiz 72
Question 4

Quiz 72
Question 6

Quiz 72
Creature Comforts

Questions	Answers
1 What kind of animal is Flower in *Bambi*?	*Skunk*
2 What kind of animal is Bullseye in the musical *Oliver*?	*Dog*
3 What kind of marine creatures are Flotsam and Jetsam in *The Little Mermaid*?	*Eels*
4 What kind of bird accompanied Mary Poppins when she sang, "A Spoonful of Sugar"?	*Robin*
5 What kind of animal is Moby Dick in the movie of the same name?	*Whale*
6 What kind of mythical creature is Mooshoo in *Mulan*?	*Dragon*
7 What kind of creature is Flik in *A Bug's Life*?	*Ant*
8 What kind of animal is Splinter, the trainer of the *Teenage Mutant Ninja Turtles*?	*Rat*
9 What kind of animal is Kala in Disney's *Tarzan*?	*Ape*
10 What kind of animal is Baloo in *The Jungle Book*?	*Bear*

Quiz 71
Question 1

Quiz 71
Question 6

Quiz 73
Dressing Room

Questions	Answers
1 What lighter-than-air substance was invented by the absent minded Professor?	*Flubber*
2 Which actor connects *Jurassic Park, Sirens* and *The Dish*?	*Sam Neill*
3 In which 1989 movie did Daniel Day-Lewis play the writer Christie Brown?	**My Left Foot**
4 The 1993 movie *Backbeat* told the story of the early days of which pop group?	*The Beatles*
5 Which outlaw was played by Paul Newman in *The Left Handed Gun*?	*Billy the Kid*
6 On which Greek island is *Zorba the Greek* set?	*Crete*
7 Which movie star played the title role in the 1998 historical drama *Elizabeth*?	*Cate Blanchett*
8 Which *Oliver* star played an outlaw in *Robin Hood, Prince of Thieves*?	*Jack Wild*
9 Who played Ferris Bueller in *Ferris Bueller's Day Off*?	**Matthew Broderick**
10 Which Disney character fell in love with a prince called Eric?	*Ariel, the Little Mermaid*

Quiz 74
Question 1

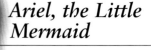

Quiz 74
Question 3

Quiz 74

In The Back Row

Questions	Answers
1 Which group performed the music for the 1980 movie *Flash Gordon*?	*Queen*
2 Who was played by Anjelica Huston in the 1991 movie *The Addams Family*?	*Morticia Addams*
3 Which musical is set in the Russian village of Anatevka?	Fiddler on the Roof
4 What surname is shared by movie stars Bruce, Christopher, Brandon and Bernard?	*Lee*
5 What is Brian's last name in *Monty Python's Life of Brian*?	*Cohen*
6 In which city did Harrison Ford search for his kidnapped wife in *Frantic*?	*Paris*
7 Which private eye created by Raymond Chandler features in *The Big Sleep*?	*Philip Marlowe*
8 Who played a welder by day and a dancer by night in *Flashdance*?	*Jennifer Beals*
9 What name connects a 1986 movie and the world's most famous painting?	*Mona Lisa*
10 Who was married to Kathleen Turner in *The War of the Roses*?	*Michael Douglas*

Quiz 73
Question 1

© Walt Disney

Quiz 75
Stage Door

Questions	Answers
1 Which star of TV's *Cheers* embarked on a murderous rampage in *Natural Born Killers*?	*Woody Harrelson*
2 Which war connects the movies *Full Metal Jacket* and *Born on the Fourth of July*?	**The Vietnam War**
3 *The Alf Garnett Saga* was a movie adaptation of which TV sitcom?	**Till Death Us Do Part**
4 *Braveheart* told of the rebellion of William Wallace against which English king?	*Edward I*
5 Which 2000 movie saw Leonardo DiCaprio on a remote Thailand island?	**The Beach**
6 Which star of TV's *Dynasty* previously starred in *The Stud* and *The Bitch*?	*Joan Collins*
7 In which 1997 movie did Jack Nicholson fall in love with Helen Hunt?	**As Good As It Gets**
8 Which actor got stung in *The Sting*, eaten by *Jaws* and killed by James Bond on a train?	*Robert Shaw*
9 In which 1995 movie were Dustin Hoffman and Rene Russo fighting a deadly virus?	**Outbreak**
10 Who played The French Lieutenant's Woman?	*Meryl Streep*

Quiz 76
Question 9

Quiz 76
Question 1

Questions	Answers
1 Who played Mel Gibson's leading lady in the comedy *Bird on a Wire*?	*Goldie Hawn*
2 Which character has been played on TV by Phil Silvers and on screen by Steve Martin?	*Sergeant Bilko*
3 Which country and western singer rode alongside John Wayne in *True Grit*?	*Glen Campbell*
4 Which political scandal was central to the 1976 movie *All the President's Men*?	*Watergate*
5 Which romantic adventure starred Catherine Zeta Jones and Antonio Banderas in 1998?	**The Mask of Zorro**
6 Which vet has been played in movies by Simon Ward and John Alderton?	*James Herriot*
7 *Il Buono, il Brutto, il Cattiva* is the Italian title of which spaghetti western?	**The Good, the Bad and the Ugly**
8 Who provided the voice of Mrs. Potts in the Disney adaptation of *Beauty and the Beast*?	*Angela Lansbury*
9 When Michael Caine played Scrooge, why was Bob Cratchit green?	*He was played by Kermit the frog*
10 Who played the title role in the 1996 movie *Michael Collins*?	*Liam Neeson*

Quiz 75
Question 5

Quiz 77
Time For Laughs

Questions	Answers
1 Which 1980 comedy starred Dolly Parton and Jane Fonda as office workers?	Nine to Five
2 In which movie did Joe Pesci play a lawyer defending his cousin in a murder trial?	My Cousin Vinny
3 Which 1974 Mel Brooks horror spoof was based on a novel by Mary Shelley?	Young Frankenstein
4 Which knighted actor played Dudley Moore's butler in the comedy *Arthur*?	*Sir John Gielgud*
5 In which movie were Matt Dillon, Ben Stiller and Lee Evans love rivals for Cameron Diaz?	There's Something About Mary
6 In which 1963 comedy were Spencer Tracy and Mickey Rooney searching for treasure?	It's a Mad Mad Mad Mad World
7 Which 1962 *Carry On* movie was set aboard a boat?	Carry On Cruising
8 In which 2000 movie did Matthew Perry play a dentist called Nicholas Oseransky?	The Whole Nine Yards
9 Which actor plays Number Two, Dr. Evil's henchman in the *Austin Powers* movies?	*Robert Wagner*
10 In which road movie did Dorothy Lamour play Princess Shalmar?	The Road to Morocco

Quiz 78
Question 4

Quiz 78
Question 7

Quiz 78
In Stitches

Questions	Answers
1 Who played Truman Burbank in the 1998 movie *The Truman Show*?	*Jim Carrey*
2 Who co-starred with Dean Martin in 16 movies between 1949 and 1956?	*Jerry Lewis*
3 Who played Mikey's mother in *Look Who's Talking*?	*Kirstie Alley*
4 Who played the bobsleigh team's coach in the movie *Cool Runnings*?	*John Candy*
5 Which military organization did Laurel and Hardy join in the movie *The Flying Deuces*?	*The Foreign Legion*
6 Who plays the heir to a $40 billion fortune in the 2002 movie, *Mr Deeds*?	*Adam Sandler*
7 In which movie did Whoopi Goldberg first play a singer called Deloris Van Cartier?	Sister Act
8 Which *Carry On* star was born Barbara Deeks?	*Barbara Windsor*
9 Which comedy actor once asked, "Who stole the cork from my breakfast?"	*W.C. Fields*
10 Who played the title role in the 1985 movie *Fletch*?	*Chevy Chase*

Quiz 77
Question 10

Quiz 79

Child Stars

Questions	Answers
1 Who sang "On the Good Ship Lollipop" in the movie *Bright Eyes*?	*Shirley Temple*
2 Who played the son of Jon Voight in the 1979 weepie *The Champ*?	*Ricky Schroder*
3 Which actor played the role of Cole in *The Sixth Sense* and a boy robot in *AI*?	*Haley Joel Osment*
4 In which 1991 movie did Macauley Culkin play the son of Jamie Lee Curtis?	**My Girl**
5 Who played Elliot's sister Gertie in *E.T.*?	*Drew Barrymore*
6 Which child star appeared with her father in the movies *Paper Moon* and *Nickelodeon*?	*Tatum O'Neal*
7 Which child actor appeared alongside Charlie Chaplin in *The Kid*?	*Jackie Coogan*
8 Which teenage star went on to play Queen Amidala in *The Phantom Menace*?	*Natalie Portman*
9 In which movie did Justin Henry play the son caught up in a child custody court case?	**Kramer versus Kramer**
10 Who won a Best Supporting Actress Oscar for her role in *The Piano*?	*Anna Paquin*

Quiz 80
Question 4

Quiz 80
Question 3

Quiz 80

21st-Century Movies

Questions	Answers
1 Which movie earned Denzel Washington a Best Actor Oscar as a streetwise cop?	**Training Day**
2 Who replaced Jodie Foster as Clarice Starling in *Hannibal*?	*Julianne Moore*
3 In which movie, set in Paris, does a poet have a passionate affair with a singer?	Moulin Rouge
4 Which 2002 war movie tells the true story of the 1965 Battle of Ia Drang Valley?	**We Were Soldiers**
5 Which movie starred Brad Pitt as an Irish gypsy boxer called Mickey O'Neil?	**Snatch**
6 Which star of TV's *The X Files* had a lead role in the comedy sci-fi *Evolution*?	*David Duchovny*
7 Who played Staff Sergeant Eversmann in the 2001 movie *Black Hawk Down*?	*Josh Harnett*
8 Which movie featured a feline called Mr. Tinkles and a puppy named Lou?	**Cats and Dogs**
9 Which martial arts hero teamed up with Chris Tucker in *Rush Hour II*?	*Jackie Chan*
10 What is the sub-title of the movie sequel *Terminator III*?	**Rise of the Machines**

Quiz 79
Question 4

Quiz 81

Opening Lines

Questions	Answers
1 Which movie opens with, "She isn't coming yet Toto. Did she hurt you?"?	The Wizard of Oz
2 Which 1985 movie opens with the line, "Professor Brown, it's almost 8.30"?	Back to the Future
3 From what movie is "It is I, Arthur, son of Uther Pendragon", one of the opening lines?	Monty Python and the Holy Grail
4 Which Hitchcock movie opens with the line, "Last night I dreamt I went to..."?	Rebecca
5 In which landmark movie did Al Jolson proclaim, "You ain't heard nothing yet"?	The Jazz Singer
6 Which Disney animation opens with the words, "Oh, I come from..."?	Aladdin
7 Which 1982 Oscar-winning epic is introduced with the words, "No man's life..."?	Gandhi
8 Which classic movie directed by and starring Orson Welles opens with a single word?	Citizen Kane
9 Which movie opens with the words spoken by the character of Benjamin Braddock?	The Graduate
10 Which movie begins with, "I believe in America. America has made my fortune..."?	The Godfather

Quiz 82
Question 6

Quiz 82
Question 8

Quiz 82
Movie Firsts

Questions	Answers
1 Who was the first actress to appear on a postage stamp?	*Grace Kelly*
2 Which all-action hero did Sylvester Stallone play in his movie debut?	*John Rambo*
3 Who first played Frankenstein's monster in movies?	*Boris Karloff*
4 Which 1995 movie was the first animated movie to be completely computer generated?	**Toy Story**
5 Which courtroom drama earned Jodie Foster her first Best Actress Oscar?	**The Accused**
6 On whose novel was *First Men in The Moon* based?	**H.G. Wells**
7 In 1987 what was the first Hollywood movie to be filmed in China?	**Empire of the Sun**
8 Who did Richard Gere portray in the 1995 movie *First Knight*?	*Sir Lancelot*
9 *The Cocoanuts* was the first movie featuring which family of actors?	*The Marx Brothers*
10 What was the title of the first James Bond movie?	**Dr. No**

Quiz 81 Question 6

Quiz 81 Question 9

Leading Ladies

Questions	Answers
1 Which star of the sitcom *Friends* played the lead in the 1997 movie *Picture Perfect*?	*Jennifer Aniston*
2 Which star of *Funny Girl* once said, "When I sing, people shut up"?	*Barbra Streisand*
3 Which wife of Orson Welles was born Margarita Carmen Cansino?	*Rita Hayworth*
4 Who played Jennifer Cavallieri in the classic *Love Story*?	*Ali McGraw*
5 Who starred in *Irma La Douce*, *Terms of Endearment* and *Two Mules for Sister Sarah*?	*Shirley MacLaine*
6 Who played the title role in the 1988 romantic comedy *Working Girl*?	*Melanie Griffith*
7 Who played Emma Peel in the 1998 movie version of *The Avengers*?	*Uma Thurman*
8 Which actress won a BAFTA and an Oscar in 1969 for her role as as Miss Jean Brodie?	*Maggie Smith*
9 With which movie star did Demi Moore walk down the aisle in 1987?	*Bruce Willis*
10 Who played the estranged wife of Robin Williams in *Mrs. Doubtfire*?	*Sally Field*

Quiz 84
Question 1

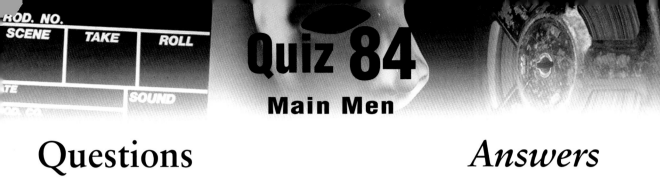

Quiz 84
Main Men

Questions	Answers
1 Which actor, born Roy Scherer, played Doris Day's leading man in *Pillow Talk*?	*Rock Hudson*
2 Who connects *Space Cowboys*, *The Client* and *The Fugitive*?	*Tommy Lee Jones*
3 Who played a doctor in *The Elephant Man* and a butler in *Remains of the Day*?	*Sir Anthony Hopkins*
4 Which movie star played the role of Grand Moff Tarkin in *Star Wars*?	*Peter Cushing*
5 Which actor interviewed Brad Pitt in *Interview with a Vampire*?	*Christian Slater*
6 Who shared the driving duties with Sandra Bullock on a booby-trapped bus in *Speed*?	*Keanu Reeves*
7 Which star of *It Happened One Night* became know as "The King of Hollywood"?	*Clark Gable*
8 Who played the cop partner of Richard Dreyfuss in the *Stake Out* movies?	*Emilio Estevez*
9 Who partnered Arnold Schwarzenegger in *Red Heat* and an Alsatian dog in *K-9*?	*James Belushi*
10 Who played the title role in the 1983 gangster movie *Scarface*?	*Al Pacino*

Quiz 83
Question 10

Quiz 85
Elvis Presley

Questions	Answers
1 Which movie sees Elvis singing in German?	**GI Blues**
2 What was the title of the movie in which he performs for a group of convicts?	**Jailhouse Rock**
3 In which movie did Elvis sing the song, "Can't Help Falling in Love"?	**Blue Hawaii**
4 Elvis played a boxer in which 1962 movie?	**Kid Galahad**
5 In which movie did Elvis play a nightclub singer called Danny Fisher?	**King Creole**
6 What was Elvis's first movie?	**Love Me Tender**
7 In which 1964 movie did he join a carnival?	**Roustabout**
8 In which 1963 movie did Elvis play both a blonde-haired and a black-haired character?	**Kissin' Cousins**
9 In which movie set in the state of Nevada did he play a sports-car racer?	**Viva Las Vegas**
10 Who played Elvis in the 1988 *Heartbreak Hotel*?	*David Keith*

Quiz 86
Question 9

Quiz 86
Charlie Chaplin

Questions	Answers
1 What nickname was given to Chaplin because of his costume in *Kid Auto Races*?	The "Little Tramp"
2 Chaplin co-founded which company with Pickford, Fairbanks and Griffith?	United Artists
3 What part of his body was insured for $150,000?	His feet
4 Who played the title role in the 1992 movie *Chaplin*?	Robert Downey Jr.
5 Did Chaplin make his first movie in 1914 or 1916?	1914
6 Which 1940 movie was a parody on Adolph Hitler?	The Great Dictator
7 In which 1936 movie did Chaplin play an assembly-line worker who goes berserk?	Modern Times
8 In which 1931 movie did he befriend a millionaire and fall in love with a blind girl?	City Lights
9 In which capital city was Chaplin born?	London
10 In which year of the 1970s did he die?	1977

Quiz 85
Question 3

Quiz 85
Question 2

Quiz 87
Clint Eastwood

Questions	Answers
1 In which movie does Eastwood play a shoe salesman who takes over a wild west show?	Bronco Billy
2 Between 1970 and 1990 how many *Dirty Harry* movies did Eastwood make?	*Five*
3 In which 1993 movie did he play a presidential bodyguard?	In the Line of Fire
4 What is the name of Eastwood's movie production company?	*Malpaso*
5 In which movie did he first appear alongside an orangutan named Clyde?	Every Which Way But Loose
6 *The Beguiled* saw a rare screen death for Eastwood after eating poisonous what?	*Mushrooms*
7 In which spaghetti western was he searching for Arch Stanton's grave?	The Good, the Bad and the Ugly
8 Which 1995 love story saw Eastwood co-starring alongside Meryl Streep?	The Bridges of Madison County
9 In 1986 Eastwood was elected Mayor of which Californian town?	*Carmel*
10 In which 1971 movie did he play a disc jockey stalked by an obsessive admirer?	Play Misty For Me

Quiz 88
Question 6

Quiz 88
Question 2

Quiz 88

Judi Dench

Questions	Answers
1 In which movie did Judi make her Bond debut as M?	Goldeneye
2 Who did she portray in *Shakespeare in Love*?	*Queen Elizabeth I*
3 Was Judi born in York, Newcastle, or Oxford?	*York*
4 Which 2000 movie saw her playing the part of Armande Voizin?	Chocolat
5 In which year of the 1980s was Judi created a Dame of the British Empire?	*1988*
6 In which adaptation of a Shakespeare play did she play Mistress Quickly?	Henry V
7 What is the title of the 2001 movie in which Judi co-stars alongside Kevin Spacey?	The Shipping News
8 In which 1999 movie did she appear with Finty Williams, Cher and Maggie Smith?	Tea with Mussolini
9 Who played Judi's husband in *Iris*?	*Jim Broadbent*
10 In which 1997 movie did she play Queen Victoria?	Mrs. Brown

Quiz 87
Question 5

Questions	Answers
1 In which 1990 movie did Robert DeNiro play the patient of Robin Williams?	Awakenings
2 Which blockbuster was about "Protecting the Earth from the scum of the Universe"?	Men in Black
3 Who starred in *Breakfast at Tiffany's* and went on to appear in *The A-Team* on TV?	*George Peppard*
4 In which movie did Sir James Bond come out of retirement to fight the SMERSH?	Casino Royale
5 Who played the vigilante Paul Kersey in the *Death Wish* movies?	*Charles Bronson*
6 Which 1995 movie earned Susan Sarandon an Oscar for her role as a nun?	Dead Man Walking
7 In which decade did Disney release *Snow White and the Seven Dwarfs*?	*1930s – in 1938*
8 Which TV police drama was adapted into a movie with Dan Aykroyd and Tom Hanks?	Dragnet
9 The movie *The Charge of the Light Brigade* was set during which war?	*Crimean War*
10 In which 1991 movie did Andrew Strong sing "Mustang Sally"?	The Commitments

Quiz 90
Question 9

Quiz 90
Question 8

Quiz 90
Matinee

Questions	Answers
1 Who played Garth in *Wayne's World*?	*Dana Carvey*
2 Which 1986 movie set during the Vietnam War won a Best Picture Oscar?	Platoon
3 Which 1962 movie told the life story of T.E. Lawrence?	Lawrence of Arabia
4 Geena Davis and Madonna played baseball teammates in which movie?	A League of their Own
5 Which 1983 movie saw Barbra Streisand disguised as a man?	Yentl
6 Who played Cornelius in the 1968 movie *Planet of the Apes*?	*Roddy McDowall*
7 In which movie did Julie Walters play a dancing teacher called Mrs. Wilkinson?	Billy Elliot
8 In which 1995 movie did James Cromwell play Farmer Arthur Hoggett?	Babe
9 Who played the title role in *Captain Corelli's Mandolin*?	*Nicholas Cage*
10 In which 1976 horror movie did Piper Laurie play Sissy Spacek's mother?	Carrie

Quiz 89
Question 4

Quiz 89
Question 9

Quiz 91

The Sound Of Music

Questions	Answers
1 Which city provided the setting for *The Sound of Music*?	*Salzburg*
2 In the movie, who plays Captain Georg von Trapp?	*Christopher Plummer*
3 Which song in the movie was performed in time to dancing and singing marionettes?	*"Lonely Goatherd"*
4 What is the first name of the character played by Julie Andrews in the movie?	*Maria*
5 Which song contains the line, "Doorbells and sleigh bells and schnitzel with noodles"?	*"My Favourite Things"*
6 Who played Mother Abbess in the movie?	*Peggy Wood*
7 How many of the Trapp children are girls?	*Five*
8 Who directed *The Sound of Music*?	*Robert Wise*
9 In the movie what is described in song as, "Small and white, clear and bright"?	*Edelweiss*
10 What is the first name of the youngest of the Trapp children?	*Gretl*

Quiz 92
Question 10

Quiz 92

In The Director's Chair

Questions	Answers
1 Which 1987 movie directed by Richard Attenborough told the story of Steve Biko?	Cry Freedom
2 Who directed the 1997 action thriller *Face/Off*?	*John Woo*
3 Which director of low-budget horror movies was played on screen by Johnny Depp?	*Ed Wood*
4 In which city does Woody Allen direct the majority of his movies?	*New York*
5 Who directed *Three Men and a Baby* and *Star Trek III*?	*Leonard Nimoy*
6 Who directed the classic *An American Werewolf in London*?	*John Landis*
7 Which star of the TV sitcom *Happy Days* directed *Splash!* and *Cocoon*?	*Ron Howard*
8 Barry Livinson directed Tom Cruise and Dustin Hoffman in which 1988 film?	**Rain Man**
9 Who directed *Staying Alive*, the 1983 sequel to *Saturday Night Fever*?	*Sylvester Stallone*
10 Which 1990 movie earned Kevin Costner an Oscar for Best Director?	**Dances With Wolves**

Quiz 91
Question 3

Quiz 93

Front Row Seats

Name the movies from the years of their release and their taglines

Questions	Answers
1 1977 – "We are not alone"	Close Encounters of the Third Kind
2 1996 – "Don't get mad, get everything"	The First Wives Club
3 1978 – "Just when you thought it was safe to go back in the water"	Jaws II
4 1999 – "Not every gift is a blessing"	The Sixth Sense
5 1967 – "They're young, they're in love and they kill people"	Bonnie and Clyde
6 1979 – "In space no one can hear you scream"	Alien
7 1994 – "Life is like a box of chocolates, you never know what you're gonna get"	Forrest Gump
8 1993 – "An adventure 65 million years in the making"	Jurassic Park
9 1978 – "The night HE came home"	Halloween
10 1997 – "If he were any cooler, he'd still be frozen, baby"	Austin Powers

Quiz 94
Question 1

Quiz 94

In The Back Row
What surname connects each group of movie stars?

Questions	Answers
1 Buster, Diane and Michael?	*Keaton*
2 Roger, Dudley and Julianne?	*Moore*
3 Nancy, Tim and Woody?	*Allen*
4 Bette, Geena and Sammy?	*Davis*
5 Richard E., Cary and Hugh?	*Grant*
6 Harold, Emily and Christopher?	*Lloyd*
7 Mimi, Roy and Ginger?	*Rogers*
8 Millicent, Steve and Dean?	*Martin*
9 Leslie, Sian and Lou Diamond?	*Phillips*
10 Danny, Julian and Crispin?	*Glover*

Quiz 93
Question 7

Quiz 95
What A Disaster!

Questions	Answers
1 Which 1975 movie told the story of an airship that exploded in 1937?	The Hindenberg
2 Which 1998 movie told the story of a comet on collision course with Earth?	Deep Impact
3 In which movie did Pierce Brosnan save Linda Hamilton from an erupting volcano?	Dante's Peak
4 Which U.S. city was destroyed in the movie *Earthquake,* starring Charlton Heston?	*Los Angeles*
5 Which disaster was recounted in the movie *A Night to Remember*?	*The sinking of the* Titanic
6 In which movie did oil driller Harry Stamper sacrifice his own life to save the world?	Armageddon
7 Which 1972 movie starring Gene Hackman took place on an ill-fated luxury cruise liner?	The Poseidon Adventure
8 Who played the role of Bill Harding in the 1996 movie *Twister*?	*Bill Paxton*
9 Who played Senator Parker in *The Towering Inferno*?	*Robert Vaughn*
10 Which peak erupted in the movie *The Last Days of Pompeii*?	*Mount Vesuvius*

Quiz 96
Question 6

Quiz 96

Tragedy And Scandal

Questions	Answers
1 Which star of the movie *Rebel Without a Cause* died in 1981 in a drowning accident?	*Natalie Wood*
2 Which co-composer for the music of *Saturday Night Fever* died in 2003?	*Maurice Gibb*
3 Who did Bridget Fonda play in the movie *Scandal*, the story of the Profumo Affair?	*Mandy Rice Davies*
4 Which movie told the story of a scandal on the TV game show *Twenty-one*?	Quiz Show
5 Who played *Hamlet* in the 1991 movie adaptation of the Shakespeare tragedy?	*Mel Gibson*
6 Which actor who starred in *Sneakers* and *Stand by Me*, died in 1993?	*River Phoenix*
7 Whose assassination in 1968 caused a delay to the Oscar ceremonies?	*Martin Luther King*
8 Which Italian-born star of *The Millionairess* was jailed in 1992?	*Sophia Loren*
9 Which silent movie star was found not guilty of killing Virginia Rappe?	*Fatty Arbuckle*
10 Which movie had James Dean just finished when he died in a car crash?	Giant

Quiz 95
Question 1

Quiz 95
Question 7

Pop Into The Movies

Questions	Answers
1 Which punk rock group made the movie *The Great Rock 'n' Roll Swindle*?	*The Sex Pistols*
2 Which member of The Who played the title role in the 1975 movie *Tommy*?	*Roger Daltrey*
3 In which movie did Tom Hanks play the manager of a group called The Oneders?	**That Thing You Do**
4 What is the surname of the All Saints' sisters who starred in *Honest*?	*Appleton*
5 Which film starring Val Kilmer featured the song "Light my Fire"?	**The Doors**
6 Which 1980s pop group performed the Bond theme for *A View to a Kill*?	*Duran Duran*
7 Who connects the movie *Out of Sight* and the hit record "If You had My Love"?	*Jennifer Lopez*
8 Name the pop superstar who starred in *The Next Best Thing*.	*Madonna*
9 In which movie did Neil Diamond play a singer called Yussel Rabinowitz?	**The Jazz Singer**
10 Which pop icon connects the movies *Performance*, *Ned Kelly* and *Freejack*?	*Mick Jagger*

Quiz 98
Question 2

Quiz 98
The Swinging 60s

Questions	Answers
1 In which U.S. city was the 1968 movie *Bullitt*, starring Steve McQueen, set?	*San Francisco*
2 Who played the title role in the 1963 movie *Cleopatra*?	*Elizabeth Taylor*
3 In which 1964 musical did Rex Harrison play Henry Higgins?	**My Fair Lady**
4 In a 1969 violent western who played the leader of The Wild Bunch?	*William Holden*
5 In which 1967 movie did Paul Newman play a convict called Lucas Jackson?	**Cool Hand Luke**
6 Which movie marked the screen farewells of Clark Gable and Marilyn Monroe?	**The Misfits**
7 Which musical featured "Ribbons down my Back" and "It Only Takes a Moment"?	**Hello Dolly**
8 Which 1966 historical drama told the story of Sir Thomas More's final years?	**A Man for All Seasons**
9 Which classic movie found Sidney Poitier investigating murder in a Mississippi town?	**In the Heat of the Night**
10 Which song from Mary Poppins won a Best Song Oscar?	*"Chim Chim Cheree"*

Quiz 97
Question 5

Quiz 97
Question 8

Quentin Tarantino

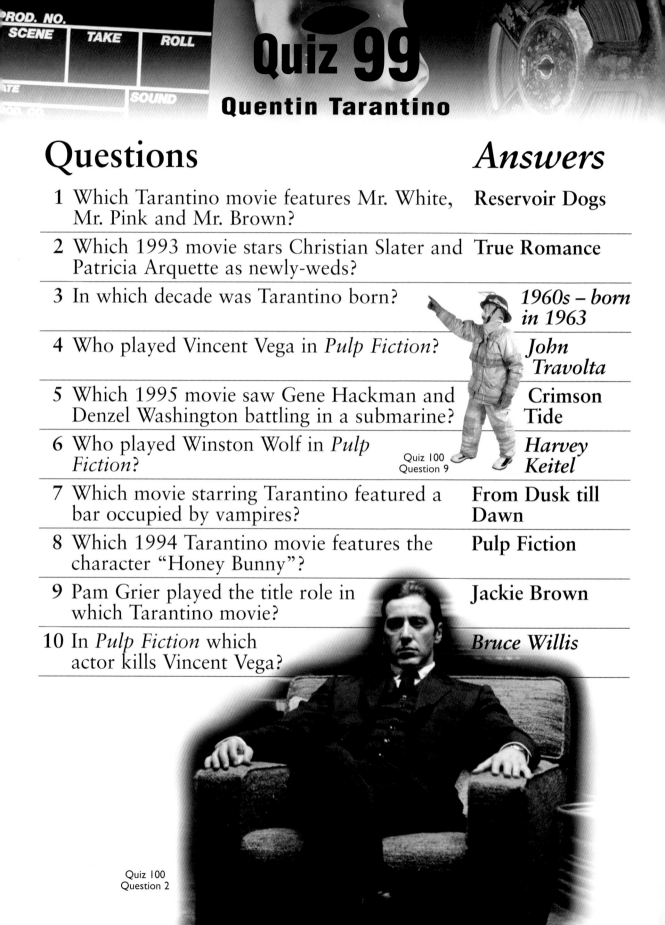

Questions	Answers
1 Which Tarantino movie features Mr. White, Mr. Pink and Mr. Brown?	Reservoir Dogs
2 Which 1993 movie stars Christian Slater and Patricia Arquette as newly-weds?	True Romance
3 In which decade was Tarantino born?	*1960s – born in 1963*
4 Who played Vincent Vega in *Pulp Fiction*?	*John Travolta*
5 Which 1995 movie saw Gene Hackman and Denzel Washington battling in a submarine?	Crimson Tide
6 Who played Winston Wolf in *Pulp Fiction*?	*Harvey Keitel*
7 Which movie starring Tarantino featured a bar occupied by vampires?	From Dusk till Dawn
8 Which 1994 Tarantino movie features the character "Honey Bunny"?	Pulp Fiction
9 Pam Grier played the title role in which Tarantino movie?	Jackie Brown
10 In *Pulp Fiction* which actor kills Vincent Vega?	*Bruce Willis*

Quiz 100
Question 9

Quiz 100
Question 2

Questions	Answers
1 In the 1996 movie *The Fan*, DeNiro plays an avid fan of which sport?	*Baseball*
2 Which movie earned him his first Best Actor Oscar?	**The Godfather Part II**
3 In which city was DeNiro born?	*New York*
4 In which movie did he play a psychotic killer called Max Cady?	Cape Fear
5 In which 1973 movie did DeNiro play the role of Johnny Boy?	Mean Streets
6 What 1989 comedy saw DeNiro and Sean Penn disguised as priests?	We're No Angels
7 Whose life story was portrayed by DeNiro in *Raging Bull*?	*Jake La Motta*
8 Who did he play in *The Untouchables*?	*Al Capone*
9 What was DeNiro's occupation in *Backdraft*?	*Firefighter*
10 In which 1995 movie was he shot dead by Al Pacino?	Heat

Quiz 99
Question 1

Quiz 101
True Stories

Questions	Answers
1 Which country was the setting for *A Cry in the Dark* starring Meryl Streep?	*Australia*
2 Which movie starring Tom Hanks told the true events of a 1970 Moon mission?	Apollo 13
3 Which movie starring Michael Caine chronicled a World War II aerial conflict?	The Battle of Britain
4 Who did Richard Attenborough portray in the movie *10 Rillington Place*?	*John Christie*
5 In which 2000 movie did Mel Gibson play Benjamin Martin?	The Patriot
6 When Laurence Olivier played Richard III, which king was played by Stanley Baker?	*Henry VII*
7 Whose autobiography was the subject of the movie *Postcards from the Edge*?	*Carrie Fisher*
8 In which movie did Nigel Hawthorne play Britain's longest reigning king?	The Madness of King George
9 Which movie starring George Clooney told the story of a boat called the *Andrea Gail*?	A Perfect Storm
10 Who played Oskar Schindler in the movie *Schindler's List*?	*Liam Neeson*

Quiz 102
Question 2

Quiz 102
Movie Sequels

Questions	Answers
1 What is the sub-title of the 1988 movie sequel *Arthur II*?	On the Rocks
2 In which movie sequel did Michael J. Fox play his own daughter?	Back to the Future II
3 What is the title of the third *Die Hard* movie?	Die Hard with a Vengeance
4 Released in 1980, what is the title of the first sequel to *Star Wars*?	The Empire Strikes Back
5 Which role was reprised by Anthony Perkins in *Psycho II*?	*Norman Bates*
6 What is the title of the 1978 sequel to *Love Story*?	Oliver's Story
7 Which 1980 horror movie spawned numerous sequels including *Jason Lives*?	Friday The 13th
8 Which 1984 comedy had six sequels by 1994 including *Citizens on Patrol*?	Police Academy
9 *The Two Jakes* was a sequel to which 1974 movie starring Jack Nicholson?	Chinatown
10 Which movie sequel followed *A Fistful of Dollars*?	For a Few Dollars More

Quiz 101
Question 1

Quiz 101
Question 10

Quiz 103
Choc Ices

Questions	Answers
1 What was the second *Harry Potter* novel to be adapted into a movie?	The Chamber of Secrets
2 In *102 Dalmatians*, what is the name of the 102nd Dalmatian?	*Oddball*
3 Shenzi and Banzai are both what kind of animals in *The Lion King*?	*Hyenas*
4 In *The Borrowers*, what drink does Pea Green dislike?	*Milk*
5 How many thieves accompany Ali Baba?	*40*
6 Which movie with a large feline cast features a sinister butler called Edgar?	The Aristocats
7 In which movie do we meet a sea witch called Ursula?	The Little Mermaid
8 Which movie character has a pet elephant called Shep, who thought he was a dog?	*George of the Jungle*
9 Which movie features the characters of Misty, Jirarudan and Ash?	**Pokémon: The First Movie**
10 Who wrote the plays on which *Hamlet* and *Henry V* are based?	*William Shakespeare*

Quiz 104
Question 3

Quiz 104
Question 7

Quiz 104
Question 8

Quiz **104**
Hot Dogs

Questions	Answers
1 What kind of dinosaurs chased two children around the kitchen in *Jurassic Park*?	*Velociraptors*
2 Which Disney movie featured a wicked witch called Maleficent?	Sleeping Beauty
3 What kind of insect attempts to be Pinocchio's conscience?	*A cricket called Jiminy Cricket*
4 Which 2001 animated movie tells the story of a white blood cell cop called Ozzy?	Osmosis Jones
5 In which movie do two dogs share a plate of spaghetti outside an Italian restaurant?	Lady and the Tramp
6 Which cartoon features a character called Chihiro whose parents are turned into pigs?	Spirited Away
7 Which Disney movie set in the jungle is based on a novel by Edgar Rice Burroughs?	Tarzan
8 *Honey, I Blew Up the Kids* is the title of the sequel to which movie?	Honey, I Shrunk the Kids
9 In which country are Bollywood movies made?	*India*
10 Which of the Muppets played Benjamina Gunn in *Muppet Treasure Island*?	*Miss Piggy*

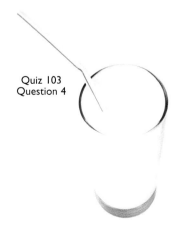

Quiz 103
Question 4

Quiz 103
Question 3

Quiz 105

Where In The World?

Name the missing places

Questions	Answers
1 *The Purple Rose of...* starring Woody Allen	Cairo
2 *Last Tango in...* starring Marlon Brando	Paris
3 *Funeral in...* starring Michael Caine	Berlin
4 *Raising...* starring Nicholas Cage	Arizona
5 *The Outlaw Josey...* starring Clint Eastwood	Wales
6 *Coming to...* starring Eddie Murphy	America
7 *Death on the...* starring Peter Ustinov	Nile
8 *The...House* starring Sean Connery	Russia
9 *The...Syndrome* starring Jane Fonda	China
10 *...Burning* starring Gene Hackman	Mississippi

Quiz 106
Question 8

Quiz 106
Question 7

Quiz 106
Animal Crackers
Name the missing creatures

Questions	Answers
1 *The…in Winter* starring Peter O'Toole	Lion
2 *A Man called…* starring Richard Harris	Horse
3 *The Day of the…* starring Edward Fox	Jackal
4 *…Day Afternoon* starring Al Pacino	Dog
5 *The Mighty…* starring Emilio Estevez	Ducks
6 *Where…Dare* starring Richard Burton	Eagles
7 *The Bad News…* starring Walter Matthau	Bears
8 *Kiss of the…Woman* starring William Hurt	Spider
9 *The Duchess and the Dirtwater…* starring George Segal	Fox
10 *…The Slayer* starring Jack Palance	Hawk

Quiz 105
Question 1

Quiz 107

Before They Were Famous

Questions	Answers
1 Which coffin polisher went on to play the world's most secret agent?	Sean Connery
2 Which star performed as a singer called Russ Le Roq in his early showbiz career?	Russell Crowe
3 As a teenager, which star played a character called Randy in the TV soap *Dallas*?	Brad Pitt
4 Which future star appeared with Brooke Shields in the movie *Endless Love*?	Tom Cruise
5 Which Oscar-winning star played Kip in the TV sitcom *Bosom Buddies*?	Tom Hanks
6 Which one of the Magnificent Seven played a wax dummy in *House of Wax*?	Charles Bronson
7 Which star danced with Bruce Springsteen in his "Dancing in the Dark" video?	Courtney Cox
8 Which future comedy star had a small role in the Dirty Harry movie, *The Dead Pool*?	Jim Carrey
9 Who was on TV in *Magnum PI* and went on to star in movies such as *Casino*?	Sharon Stone
10 Which Oscar-winning actor was born Kevin Fowler?	Kevin Spacey

Quiz 108
Question 8

Quiz 108
Rocky

Questions	Answers
1 How many *Rocky* movies were made in the 20th century?	*Five*
2 Who plays Rocky's brother-in-law Paulie in the movies?	*Burt Young*
3 Which pop group recorded the *Rocky* theme, "Eye of the Tiger"?	*Survivor*
4 Which star of *The A-Team* played the brutal boxer Clubber Lang in *Rocky III*?	*Mr. T*
5 Which U.S. city is the home city of Rocky?	*Philadelphia*
6 In the *Rocky* movies, who plays his supportive girlfriend and wife, Adrian?	*Talia Shire*
7 What is the name of the boxer played by Carl Weathers in the *Rocky* movies?	*Apollo Creed*
8 Who played the Russian boxer Ivan Drago in *Rocky IV*?	*Dolph Lungren*
9 Who directed the 1976 movie *Rocky*?	*John G. Avildsen*
10 What is Rocky's last name?	*Balboa*

Quiz 107
Question 3

Nicole Kidman

Questions	Answers
1 In which 1993 movie does Nicole play Michael Keaton's pregnant wife?	My Life
2 On which island was she born?	*Hawaii*
3 In which 1998 movie do Nicole and Sandra Bullock dabble in witchcraft?	Practical Magic
4 Who directed Nicole in *Eyes Wide Shut*?	*Stanley Kubrick*
5 In which movie does she play a murderous TV reporter, Suzanne Maretto?	To Die For
6 What was the title of the first movie in which Nicole co-starred with Tom Cruise?	Days of Thunder
7 In which 1988 thriller did she play Sam Neill's wife?	Dead Calm
8 Nicole played Dr. Chase Meridian in which movie?	Batman Forever
9 In which movie did she play Dustin Hoffman's moll?	Billy Bathgate
10 In which year did Nicole marry Tom Cruise?	*1990*

Quiz 110
Question 9

Quiz 110
Tom Cruise

Questions	Answers
1 What is the name of the character that Cruise plays in the *Mission Impossible* movies?	*Ethan Hunt*
2 In which 1992 movie did he cross-examine Jack Nicholson in a military courtroom?	**A Few Good Men**
3 Which movie sees Cruise mixing Pina Coladas and Harvey Wallbangers?	Cocktail
4 What was Cruise's pilot call sign in *Top Gun*?	*Maverick*
5 In which movie, based on a John Grisham novel, did he play a Mafia lawyer?	The Firm
6 Who was he married to from 1987 to 1990?	*Mimi Rogers*
7 Which actress starred with Cruise in *Jerry Maguire*?	*Renee Zellwegger*
8 In which 2002 futuristic thriller does Cruise play Chief John Anderton?	**Minority Report**
9 Which movie earned him his first Oscar nomination?	**Born on the Fourth of July**
10 What is Cruise's real surname?	*Mapother*

Quiz 109
Question 2

Quiz 109
Question 8

Quiz 111

Preview

Questions	Answers
1 Who played Perry in *Kevin & Perry Go Large*?	*Kathy Burke*
2 In which country was *The Killing Fields* set?	*Cambodia*
3 What is the first name of Baron Frankenstein?	*Victor*
4 What connects *Raising Cain* and *The Man in the Iron Mask*?	**Twin brothers**
5 In which 1985 comedy did Richard Pryor inherit millions of dollars?	**Brewster's Millions**
6 In which movie with Nicholas Cage and John Travolta did Archer "borrow" Troy's face?	**Face/Off**
7 Which movie found David Tomlinson "on the bottom of the beautiful briny sea"?	**Bedknobs and Broomsticks**
8 Which of the Marx Brothers was born with the first name of Leonard?	*Chico*
9 In which 1995 movie did Michelle Pfeiffer become an inner-city schoolteacher?	**Dangerous Minds**
10 The 1993 movie *Dragon* is a biopic of which martial arts hero?	*Bruce Lee*

Quiz 112
Question 6

Quiz 112
Question 4

Quiz 112
Matinee

Questions	Answers
1 Who connects the epics *Lawrence of Arabia*, *Ulysses* and *Barabbas*?	*Anthony Quinn*
2 Who has been played on screen by Bo Derek, Dorothy Dunbar and Maureen O'Sullivan?	*Tarzan's Jane*
3 Who played the President of the U.S.A. in *Primary Colors*?	*John Travolta*
4 How are Curly, Larry and Mo collectively known?	*The Three Stooges*
5 Who played Oscar Madison in *The Odd Couple*?	*Walter Matthau*
6 What game is played by Steve McQueen and Faye Dunaway in *The Thomas Crown Affair*?	*Chess*
7 Who was the first British star to win a Best Actress Oscar?	*Vivien Leigh*
8 Who played Henry VIII in *Carry On Henry*?	*Sid James*
9 Which writer did Virginia McKenna portray in *Born Free*?	*Joy Adamson*
10 In *Peter's Friends* which British comedy star played Peter?	*Stephen Fry*

Quiz 111
Question 5

Quiz 113

Black Comedy

Questions	Answers
1 Which black comedy starred Kevin Spacey and Annette Bening as a bickering couple?	**American Beauty**
2 Who played Dr. Strangelove in the 1964 movie?	*Peter Sellers*
3 In which 1986 picture did Judge Reinhold and Helen Slater kidnap Bette Midler?	**Ruthless People**
4 In Alfred Hitchcock's *The Trouble with Harry*, what was Harry's trouble?	*A corpse*
5 Which 1996 movie set in Scotland features the characters of Spud, Renton and Begbie?	**Trainspotting**
6 During which war was *Catch 22* set?	*World War II*
7 Who played the role of Martin Weir in the black comedy *Get Shorty*?	*Danny DeVito*
8 In which movie did Frances McDormand play a pregnant police chief?	**Fargo**
9 Who played Hannah in the Woody Allen comedy *Hannah and Her Sisters*?	*Mia Farrow*
10 In which movie classic did Alec Guinness play eight members of the d'Ascoyne family?	**Kind Hearts and Coronets**

Quiz 114
Question 1

Quiz 114
Question 3

Quiz 114
Foreign Movies

Questions	Answers
1 Which German screen icon played the leading lady in *The Blue Angel*?	*Marlene Dietrich*
2 Who directed *Crouching Tiger, Hidden Dragon*?	*Ang Lee*
3 In which capital city is Frederico Fellini's *La Dolce Vita* set?	*Rome*
4 Which 1922 horror classic sees Max Schreck playing a vampire?	**Nosferatu**
5 On which Shakespeare play was the Japanese movie *Ran* based?	**King Lear**
6 *The Magnificent Seven* was based on which classic foreign movie?	**The Seven Samurai**
7 In which 1956 movie did Max von Sydow play a knight returning from the Crusades?	**The Seventh Seal**
8 Which French actor played the title role in *Monsieur Hulot's Holiday*?	*Jacques Tati*
9 Which French pin-up connects *Viva Maria*, *Vie Privée* and *Helen of Troy*?	*Brigitte Bardot*
10 Who played the title rolc in the 2001 Oscar nominated movie *Amelie*?	*Audrey Tautou*

Quiz 113
Question 6

Quiz 113
Question 7

Quiz 115

Novel Ideas

Questions	Answers
1 On whose novel was the 1968 horror *The Devil Rides Out* based?	*Dennis Wheatley*
2 Which movie based on George Orwell's novel was Richard Burton's final role?	1984
3 In which adaptation of a Dickens' novel did Jean Cadell play Mrs. Micawber?	**David Copperfield**
4 Which war movie co-starring Lee Marvin, was based on a novel by E.M. Nathanson?	**The Dirty Dozen**
5 Who wrote the novels from which *Watership Down* and *The Plague Dogs* were adapted?	*Richard Adams*
6 Who played Fagin in the 1968 movie version of Charles Dickens' novel *Oliver Twist*?	*Ron Moody*
7 Which F. Scott Fitzgerald novel was remade in 1974 starring Robert Redford?	**The Great Gatsby**
8 Whose novel *A Clockwork Orange* was adapted into a controversial movie?	*Anthony Burgess*
9 What is the title of the novel on which the Oscar-winning movie *Schindler's List* is based?	Schindler's Ark
10 Which Robert Louis Stevenson novel, filmed in 1960, features a hero called David Balfour?	Kidnapped

Quiz 116
Question 2

Quiz 116
Road Movies

Questions	Answers
1 In which 1965 picture did Jack Lemmon play the evil Professor Fate?	The Great Race
2 In which 1978 movie did Kris Kristofferson use the call sign Rubber Duck?	Convoy
3 Which 1991 road movie saw Michael Madsen play Susan Sarandon's boyfriend?	Thelma and Louise
4 Who played Smokey in the 1977 movie *Smokey and the Bandit*?	*Jackie Gleason*
5 Which 1981 comedy tells the story of a road race from Connecticut to California?	The Cannonball Run
6 What was the last road movie made by Bob Hope and Bing Crosby, filmed in 1962?	Road to Hong Kong
7 Which movie featured Whoopi Goldberg and Drew Barrymore driving across the U.S.A.?	Boys on the Side
8 In which 1954 picture did Marlon Brando play the leader of a motorcycle gang?	The Wild One
9 Chevy Chase, John Belushi and Emilio Estevez have each starred in which series of movies?	National Lampoon's
10 Who played Captain America in *Easy Rider*?	*Peter Fonda*

Quiz 115
Question 6

Quiz 117

Popcorn
What is the name of...

Questions	Answers
1 The car in *The Love Bug*?	*Herbie*
2 The prospector in *Toy Story II*?	*Stinky Pete*
3 The baby son of Barney Rubble?	*Bam Bam*
4 The evil uncle in *The Lion King*?	*Scar*
5 The fairy in *Peter Pan*?	*Tinkerbell*
6 The one-legged pirate in *Treasure Island*?	*Long John Silver*
7 The female mouse in *The Rescuers*?	*Bianca*
8 The pet dog of *The Grinch*?	*Max*
9 The town ruled by Lord Farquaad in *Shrek*?	*Duloc*
10 The Emperor in *The Emperor's New Groove*	*Kuzco*

Quiz 118
Question 2

Quiz 118

Questions	Answers
1 Popeye's archenemy?	*Bluto*
2 The gang of children in Never Never Land?	*The Lost Boys*
3 The droid played by Kenny Baker in *Star Wars*?	*R2-D2*
4 Dumbo the elephant's mother?	*Mrs. Jumbo*
5 The eldest son of Gomez and Morticia Addams?	*Pugsley*
6 The panther in *The Jungle Book*?	*Bagheera*
7 The group of miners who sang, "Heigh Ho"?	*Seven Dwarfs*
8 The character played by Linda Cardellini in *Scooby Doo*?	*Velma*
9 Juni's sister in *Spy Kids*?	*Carmen*
10 The magical flying white horse in *Hercules*?	*Pegasus*

Quiz 117
Question 10

Quiz 117
Question 5

Quiz 119

Epics

Questions	Answers
1 In which movie did Kirk Douglas play a Norse warrior called Einar?	The Vikings
2 Which 1959 epic saw Charlton Heston competing in a chariot race?	Ben Hur
3 Cecil B. de Mille made two versions of which biblical epic?	The Ten Commandments
4 Which goddess did Honor Blackman play in *Jason and the Argonauts*?	*Hera*
5 Who played Samson in the 1950 epic *Samson and Delilah*?	*Victor Mature*
6 Which 1960 movie tells the story of a Roman slave who led a slave's revolt?	Spartacus
7 Which Emperor was played by Peter Ustinov in *Quo Vadis*?	*The Emperor Nero*
8 Which epic of the 1930s was billed as, "Margaret Mitchell's story of the Old South"?	Gone with the Wind
9 On whose novel was the 1984 movie *A Passage to India* based?	*E.M. Forster*
10 Who plays Count Almasy in the 1996 Oscar-winning *The English Patient*?	*Ralph Fiennes*

Quiz 120
Question 1

Quiz 120
Question 8

Questions

1 Which studio made the *Carry On* movies?

2 What is the name of the lion that appears in the opening credits of all MGM movies?

3 A mountain peak surrounded by stars is the logo of which studio?

4 Why was the sorcerer called Yensid in the animated movie *Fantasia*?

5 "The Proud Lady" is the nickname given to which movie studio's logo?

6 Which London studios made *The Lavender Hill Mob* and *The Blue Lamp*?

7 Four siblings called Albert, Harry, Jack and Sam founded which studio?

8 The British company Hammer Films is known for making which genre of movies?

9 Which company founded in 1912 announced a $65 million loss in 1998?

10 Which studio made the animated movie *Chicken Run*?

Answers

Pinewood Studios

Leo

Paramount

Yensid is Disney spelt backwards

Columbia

Ealing Studios

Warner Brothers

Horror movies

Universal Studios

DreamWorks

Quiz 119
Question 8

Quiz 121
The Wizard Of Oz

Questions	Answers
1 What is the name of Dorothy's dog in *The Wizard of Oz*?	*Toto*
2 Which U.S. state is home to Dorothy?	*Kansas*
3 In the movie what is the name of the cowardly lion?	*Zeke*
4 Which race of small people advised Dorothy to "follow the yellow brick road"?	*Munchkins*
5 Which character was portrayed by Ray Bolger?	*The Scarecrow*
6 What is the name of Dorothy's aunt in *The Wizard of Oz*?	*Auntie Em*
7 What does Dorothy say three times when she taps the heels of her ruby slippers together?	*"There's no place like home"*
8 On whose novel is the movie based?	*L. Frank Baum*
9 Name the actor who played the Wizard of Oz.	*Frank Morgan*
10 To which city does Dorothy travel to meet the "wonderful Wizard of Oz"?	*The Emerald City*

Quiz 122
Question 6

Quiz 122
Question 1

Questions

Answers

	Questions	Answers
1	In *The Great Escape* who attempted to escape from his pursuers on a motorcycle?	*Steve McQueen*
2	Name the actor who the played the "Tunnel King" and suffered from claustrophobia.	*Charles Bronson*
3	Which actor was shot in the back on a railway line whilst attempting to escape?	*David McCallum*
4	What code name was given to the character played by Richard Attenborough?	*Big X*
5	In *The Great Escape*, who played "The Forger"?	*Donald Pleasance*
6	What was the nationality of the character played by James Coburn in the movie?	*Australian*
7	Which Scottish actor played the intelligence officer at the P.O.W. camp?	*Gordon Jackson*
8	What code name was given to the three escape tunnels?	*Tom, Dick and Harry*
9	Who played the "Scrounger" in the movie?	*James Garner*
10	Who directed *The Great Escape*?	*John Sturges*

Quiz 121
Question 5

Quiz 121
Question 10

Quiz 123
At The Flicks

Questions	Answers
1 Which star of the TV series *The Young Ones*, played Fred in *Drop Dead Fred*?	*Rik Mayall*
2 In which 1997 thriller did Brad Pitt play a terrorist called Frankie Maguire?	**The Devil's Own**
3 What is the title of the fourth movie to feature the character of Hannibal Lecter?	**Red Dragon**
4 For which comedy did a choir mistress called Iris Stevenson provide the inspiration?	Sister Act
5 Who played Sergeant Emil Foley in *An Officer and a Gentleman*?	*Louis Gossett Jr.*
6 In *E.T.*, a spacecraft abandons E.T. in the suburbs of which U.S. city?	*Los Angeles*
7 In which 1985 thriller did Glenn Close defend Jeff Bridges against a murder charge?	**Jagged Edge**
8 In the movie *Three Men and a Baby*, who played the character called Pete Mitchell?	*Tom Selleck*
9 Which of the Marx Brothers shares his name with Oprah Winfrey's production company?	*Harpo*
10 Who died in *The Towering Inferno* and went on to star in the TV series *Hart to Hart*?	*Robert Wagner*

Quiz 124
Question 8

Quiz 124
Stage Door

Questions	Answers
1 In which musical did Clint Eastwood co-star with Jean Seberg?	**Paint Your Wagon**
2 In which movie did Jack Nicholson share a bedroom scene with Michelle Pfeiffer?	**The Witches of Eastwick**
3 Name the political activist killed in 1922 and played on screen by Liam Neeson.	*Michael Collins*
4 Which country holds a festival that awards The Golden Bear to the best movie?	*Germany*
5 On screen Robert Redford and Paul Newman carried out "The Sting" in which city?	*Chicago*
6 In which 1999 picture does Sean Connery attempt to steal a priceless Chinese mask?	**Entrapment**
7 What is the surname of the owners of the chicken farm in *Chicken Run*?	*Tweedy*
8 In which movie did Demi Moore shave off her hair when joining the U.S. Navy Seals?	**GI Jane**
9 In which musical did Richard Harris portray King Arthur?	**Camelot**
10 In which century was the epic *El Cid* set?	*11th century*

Quiz 123
Question 8

Quiz 123
Question 2

Quiz 125
Potter Mania

Questions	Answers
1 From which London train station does the *Hogwart's Express* depart?	King's Cross
2 Who plays Harry Potter?	Daniel Radcliffe
3 Which actor played the Albus Dumbedore in the first two movies?	Richard Harris
4 What was *Harry Potter and the Philosopher's Stone* called in the U.S.?	Harry Potter and the Sorcerer's Stone
5 What is the name of Harry Potter's uncle, played on screen by Richard Griffiths?	Vernon
6 In the *Harry Potter* movies, who is portrayed by Rupert Grint?	Ron Weasley
7 Who plays the character of Gilderoy Lockhart in the second *Harry Potter* movie?	Kenneth Branagh
8 What is the name of the professor played by Alan Rickman?	Professor Severus Snape
9 What is Hagrid's three-headed dog called?	Fluffy
10 Is the *Hogwart's Express* black, red or green?	Red

Quiz 126
Question 6

Quiz 126
Question 3

Quiz 126
Question 7

Quiz 126

101 Dalmatians

Questions	Answers
1 What breed of dog is the Colonel in the animated movie?	*Old English sheepdog*
2 In the cartoon movie what is the name of the Dalmatian puppy that is forever hungry?	*Rolly*
3 Who does Glenn Close portray in the live-action version of the story?	*Cruella DeVil*
4 In the Disney animation what is the name of the dog who fathers the Dalmatians?	*Pongo*
5 What is the name of the cat who helps the Dalmatians escape from their kidnappers?	*Sergeant Tibbs*
6 What did Princess and Duchess give to the Dalmatians on their travels?	*Milk – they are both cows*
7 What type of bird is Lucy in the cartoon version?	*Goose*
8 How does Roger earn his living in *101 Dalmatians*?	*As a songwriter*
9 In the Disney cartoon, what is the name of Roger's wife?	*Anita*
10 Who wrote the novel on which the movies are based?	*Dodie Smith*

Quiz 125
Question 3

Quiz 125
Question 6

Quiz 127
Movie Buffs

Questions	Answers
1 Which 2001 comedy included appearances by Jeffrey Archer and Salman Rushdie?	Bridget Jones's Diary
2 Which Nazi was portrayed by Gregory Peck in *The Boys from Brazil*?	*Josef Mengele*
3 In which movie did Nick Nolte fall in love with Barbra Streisand?	The Prince of Tides
4 Who was the only English-born actor to win a Best Actor Oscar in the 1990s?	*Jeremy Irons*
5 When Alec Guinness portrayed Fagin who played Bill Sikes?	*Robert Newton*
6 When Errol Flynn played Robin Hood who did Alan Hale portray?	*Little John*
7 Which war movie told the story of the German counter-attack in the Ardennes?	The Battle of the Bulge
8 In a Disney movie whose voices were provided by Paige O'Hara and Robby Benson?	Beauty and the Beast
9 In 1932, which European city hosted the world's first movie festival?	*Venice*
10 Who played Tarzan when Bo Derek played Jane?	*Miles O'Keefe*

Quiz 128
Question 6

Quiz 128
Question 3

Quiz 128
Tough Trivia

Questions	Answers
1 What was the first X-rated movie to win the Best Picture Oscar?	**Midnight Cowboy**
2 What was the name of the newspaper that Kane owned and ran in *Citizen Kane*?	**The Inquirer**
3 Which movie star became the first stepmother to Carrie Fisher?	*Elizabeth Taylor*
4 Which 1987 movie starring Oliver Reed was based on Lucy Irving's autobiography?	**Castaway**
5 Which pop star replaced Michael Caine as Alfie in the 1975 sequel *Alfie Darling*?	*Alan Price*
6 What part was played by both Cary Grant and Michael Hordern in *Alice in Wonderland*?	*Mock Turtle*
7 Who narrated the 1993 western *Tombstone*, starring Kurt Russell as Wyatt Earp?	*Robert Mitchum*
8 The 1996 movie *The Birdcage* was a remake of which French movie?	**La Cage aux Folles**
9 In which U.S. state was *The Blair Witch Project* set?	*Maryland*
10 In which century was the sci-fi fantasy *Barbarella* set?	*40th century*

Quiz 127
Question 1

Quiz 127
Question 9

Fantasy

Questions	Answers
1 Which 1984 fantasy saw the character of Bastian entering the land of Fantasia?	The Never Ending Story
2 In which 1982 movie did John Cleese play Robin Hood and Ian Holm play Napoleon?	Time Bandits
3 What was the title of the movie in which David Bowie played the evil Goblin King?	Labyrinth
4 Which movie tells the story of an orphan raised by a group called the Mystics?	The Dark Crystal
5 In which 1988 movie did Val Kilmer play a swashbuckling warrior called Madmartigan?	Willow
6 Laurence Olivier played the Greek God Zeus in which 1981 classic?	Clash of the Titans
7 Who played opposite Cyd Charisse in the 1954 musical *Brigadoon*?	Gene Kelly
8 Nigel Terry played King Arthur in which 1981 movie?	Excalibur
9 Which 1987 fantasy featured cameo appearances by Peter Falk and Billy Crystal?	The Princess Bride
10 In which 1990 movie did Johnny Depp possess metal hands?	Edward Scissorhands

Quiz 130
Question 8

Quiz 130
A Fine Romance

Questions	Answers
1 Robert Redford and Barbra Streisand played lovers in which 1973 picture?	The Way We Were
2 In which 1991 movie did Al Pacino play a cook who woos waitress Michelle Pfeiffer?	Frankie and Johnny
3 In the Cary Grant romantic comedy *Bringing up Baby*, what kind of wild cat is Baby?	*Leopard*
4 In which 1984 movie did Tom Hanks fall in love with a mermaid?	Splash!
5 Who romanced Humphrey Bogart in *To Have and Have Not* and then married him?	*Lauren Bacall*
6 Which movie star died in 1926 after appearing in *The Sheik and the Eagle*?	*Rudolph Valentino*
7 In which 1987 picture did Nicholas Cage confess, "I'm in love with you" to Cher?	Moonstruck
8 Where did Celia Johnson and Trevor Howard conduct a love affair in *Brief Encounter*?	*At a train station*
9 Who played Shakespeare in the 1998 movie *Shakespeare in Love*?	*Joseph Fiennes*
10 Who played the bride in the 1997 romantic comedy *My Best Friend's Wedding*?	*Cameron Diaz*

Quiz 129
Question 7

Quiz 131

B movies

Questions	Answers
1 In which movie did Woody Allen find himself embroiled in a South American rebellion?	**Bananas**
2 Which Gene Kelly musical features the song, "The Heather on the Hill"?	**Brigadoon**
3 In which 2000 comedy did Brendan Fraser sign away his soul to the devil?	**Bedazzled**
4 Which animated deer was introduced to the big screen in 1942 by the Disney studios?	**Bambi**
5 In which 1996 movie did David Bowie portray Andy Warhol?	**Basquiat**
6 Which 1995 movie told the story of an orphaned piglet adopted by a sheepdog?	**Babe**
7 Which 1997 comedy was directed by Mel Smith and co-starred John Mills?	**Bean**
8 In which 1988 picture did Robert Loggia play Tom Hanks' boss?	**Big**
9 What is the title of the 1992 movie that starred a St. Bernard dog?	**Beethoven**
10 Which 1989 movie was set in Gotham City?	**Batman**

Quiz 132
Question 8

Quiz 132
Matinee

Questions	Answers
1 In which 2002 movie does Paul Newman play a Mafia boss called John Rooney?	*The Road to Perdition*
2 Who was nominated for a Best Actor Oscar for his role in the *The Stuntman?*	*Peter O'Toole*
3 Who played a sleazy investigator in the comedy *There's Something about Mary?*	*Matt Dillon*
4 Which actor played the lead role in the 1990 flop *Almost an Angel?*	*Paul Hogan*
5 Which Canadian-born star married Douglas Fairbanks Sr.?	*Mary Pickford*
6 Who composed the theme for the Bond movie, *Live and Let Die?*	*Paul McCartney*
7 Which 1977 Disney movie featured a dragon called Elliot?	**Pete's Dragon**
8 In which movie did Karen Dotrice play Jane Banks?	**Mary Poppins**
9 On whose novel was *Jaws* based?	**Peter Benchley**
10 Who played Clouseau in *The Pink Panther?*	*Peter Sellers*

Quiz 131
Question 1

Quiz 131
Question 9

Superman

Questions	Answers
1 Who played Lex Luthor in three *Superman* movies?	*Gene Hackman*
2 In what year was Christopher Reeve paralyzed in a horse-riding accident?	*1995*
3 Who played the evil villain Zod in *Superman II*?	*Terence Stamp*
4 What newspaper does Clark Kent work for?	**The Daily Planet**
5 Which actor plays Otis, Lex Luthor's hapless sidekick?	*Ned Beatty*
6 Who received a reported $3 million fee for a ten-minute appearance as Superman's father?	*Marlon Brando*
7 Which British actress played Superman's mother in *Superman II*?	*Susannah York*
8 Which character is played by Margot Kidder in the *Superman* movies?	*Lois Lane*
9 What was the subtitle of *Superman IV*?	**The Quest for Peace**
10 Who composed the music for the 1978 movie?	*John Williams*

Quiz 134
Question 4

Quiz 134
Question 9

Quiz 132

Matinee

Questions	Answers
1 In which 2002 movie does Paul Newman play a Mafia boss called John Rooney?	*The Road to Perdition*
2 Who was nominated for a Best Actor Oscar for his role in the *The Stuntman?*	*Peter O'Toole*
3 Who played a sleazy investigator in the comedy *There's Something about Mary?*	*Matt Dillon*
4 Which actor played the lead role in the 1990 flop *Almost an Angel?*	*Paul Hogan*
5 Which Canadian-born star married Douglas Fairbanks Sr.?	*Mary Pickford*
6 Who composed the theme for the Bond movie, *Live and Let Die?*	*Paul McCartney*
7 Which 1977 Disney movie featured a dragon called Elliot?	Pete's Dragon
8 In which movie did Karen Dotrice play Jane Banks?	Mary Poppins
9 On whose novel was *Jaws* based?	*Peter Benchley*
10 Who played Clouseau in *The Pink Panther?*	*Peter Sellers*

Quiz 131
Question 1

Quiz 131
Question 9

Quiz 133

Superman

Questions	Answers
1 Who played Lex Luthor in three *Superman* movies?	*Gene Hackman*
2 In what year was Christopher Reeve paralyzed in a horse-riding accident?	*1995*
3 Who played the evil villain Zod in *Superman II*?	*Terence Stamp*
4 What newspaper does Clark Kent work for?	**The Daily Planet**
5 Which actor plays Otis, Lex Luthor's hapless sidekick?	*Ned Beatty*
6 Who received a reported $3 million fee for a ten-minute appearance as Superman's father?	*Marlon Brando*
7 Which British actress played Superman's mother in *Superman II*?	*Susannah York*
8 Which character is played by Margot Kidder in the *Superman* movies?	*Lois Lane*
9 What was the subtitle of *Superman IV*?	**The Quest for Peace**
10 Who composed the music for the 1978 movie?	*John Williams*

Quiz 134
Question 9

Quiz 134
Question 4

Batman

Questions	Answers
1 Who played Batman in the 1989 movie *Batman* and in *Batman Returns* in 1992?	*Michael Keaton*
2 Which star of the 2000 movie *Charlie's Angels* played Sugar in *Batman Forever*?	*Drew Barrymore*
3 Who played Batgirl in *Batman and Robin*?	*Alicia Silverstone*
4 How is the character of Oswald Cobblepot better known?	*The Penguin*
5 What is the name of the villain played by Tommy Lee Jones in *Batman Forever*?	*Two-Face*
6 Who played Batman in the 1966 picture and the 1960s TV series?	*Adam West*
7 Which foe of Batman was portrayed on screen by Arnold Schwarzenegger?	*Mr. Freeze*
8 Which character was played on TV by Burt Ward and on screen by Chris O'Donnell?	*Robin*
9 Who played newspaper reporter Vicki Vale in the 1989 *Batman* movie?	*Kim Basinger*
10 Who directed the 1989 movie and its 1992 sequel?	*Tim Burton*

Quiz 133
Question 8

Quiz 133
Question 6

Quiz 135

Stage Door

Questions	Answers
1 What is the title of the 1999 sequel to *Gregory's Girl*?	Gregory's Two Girls
2 Which actor connects *The Wild Geese*, *Gold* and *Shout at the Devil*?	*Roger Moore*
3 Which star received the Irving Thalberg Award at the 2000 Oscar ceremonies?	*Warren Beatty*
4 Hugh Hudson directed which Oscar-winning picture of the 1980s?	Chariots of Fire
5 Who did Dennis Quaid portray in *Great Balls of Fire*?	*Jerry Lee Lewis*
6 Which 1992 movie featured the characters of Uncas, Chingachgook and Hawkeye?	The Last of the Mohicans
7 Which musical features a man-eating plant called Audrey II?	Little Shop of Horrors
8 Who played the role of M in the 1983 Bond movie, *Never Say Never Again*?	*Edward Fox*
9 Which musical features "The Time Warp"?	The Rocky Horror Picture Show
10 Which star of the TV series *Starsky and Hutch* directed *The Running Man*?	*Paul Michael Glaser*

Quiz 136
Question 8

Quiz 136
At The Flicks

Questions	Answers
1 Which actress connects *Copycat*, *Dave* and *Working Girl*?	*Sigourney Weaver*
2 Which British Dame won an Oscar for her role in *A Passage to India*?	*Peggy Ashcroft*
3 Which novel by Tom Wolfe was turned into a movie starring Tom Hanks and Bruce Willis?	**Bonfire of the Vanities**
4 Which 1990 picture featured a pair of hapless burglars called Harry and Marv?	**Home Alone**
5 Who sang the theme for the 1984 movie, *Footloose*?	*Kenny Loggins*
6 In *The Lion King* who wrote the lyrics for the Oscar-winning song, "Circle of Life"?	*Tim Rice*
7 Meryl Streep played Karen Blixen in which 1985 Oscar-winning picture?	**Out of Africa**
8 Which 1962 musical sees Cliff Richard driving a double-decker bus?	**Summer Holiday**
9 Which 1978 movie starring Barbra Streisand had been made in 1937 and again in 1954?	**A Star is Born**
10 Which 1978 musical is set at Rydell High School?	**Grease**

Quiz 135
Question 4

Quiz 137
Robin Williams

Questions	Answers
1 In which movie did Williams find himself imprisoned in a board game?	**Jumanji**
2 He earned his first Oscar nomination for which picture?	**Good Morning Vietnam**
3 What is the title of the 1999 movie in which Williams plays a robot?	**Bicentennial Man**
4 In what decade was he born?	*1950s – born in 1952*
5 When Williams played Popeye who played Olive Oyl?	*Shelley Duvall*
6 Which movie, based on a true story, saw him playing an unconventional doctor?	**Patch Adams**
7 Which 1997 picture earned Williams a Best Supporting Actor Oscar?	**Good Will Hunting**
8 Williams sings "Friend like me" in which 1992 movie?	**Aladdin,** *as the voice of the Genie*
9 In which picture does he play a tramp who was once a medieval historian?	**The Fisher King**
10 DEPOSITED TEA COSY is an anagram of which movie starring Williams?	**Dead Poets Society**

Quiz 138
Question 1

Quiz 138

Julia Roberts

Questions	Answers
1 Julia co-starred with Richard Gere for the second time in which movie?	**Runaway Bride**
2 Beginning with F, what is Julia's middle name?	*Fiona*
3 In which 1991 fantasy did she play Tinkerbell?	Hook
4 In which 1997 movie is Mel Gibson helped by Julia to overcome his paranoia?	Conspiracy Theory
5 Which 2000 picture earned Julia her first Best Actress Oscar?	**Erin Brockovich**
6 Which actor became engaged to Julia in 1990?	*Kiefer Sutherland*
7 In the movie *Sleeping with the Enemy*, who played her abusive husband?	*Patrick Bergin*
8 What is the first name of the character played by Julia in *Pretty Woman*?	*Vivian*
9 MIX THE CANE is an anagram of which movie starring Julia?	The Mexican
10 Who did she marry in 2002?	*Danny Moder*

Quiz 137
Question 1

Quiz 139

Dressing Room

Unravel the anagrams to give the name of a famous male movie star

Questions	Answers
1 PROFANE TED	*Peter Fonda*
2 BURRLY MAIL	*Bill Murray*
3 BEWARE TYRANT	*Warren Beatty*
4 A LION CAP	*Al Pacino*
5 DUPED MY HEIR	*Eddie Murphy*
6 OLD WEST ACTION	*Clint Eastwood*
7 BIG MELONS	*Mel Gibson*
8 SEAL COACHING	*Nicholas Cage*
9 MOIST CURE	*Tom Cruise*
10 BLAST CRY LILY	*Billy Crystal*

Quiz 140
Question 10

Stage Door

Unravel the anagrams to give the name of a famous female movie star

Questions	Answers
1 HEALING JET	*Janet Leigh*
2 DIETS FOR JOE	*Jodie Foster*
3 DREAM BRINGING	*Ingrid Bergman*
4 MERRY WARDROBE	*Drew Barrymore*
5 HONEST ARSON	*Sharon Stone*
6 LEN THE HUN	*Helen Hunt*
7 SAME WET	*Mae West*
8 BATH AT KEYS	*Kathy Bates*
9 A NEWEST KILT	*Kate Winslet*
10 DO DIARYS	*Doris Day*

Quiz 139
Question 5

Quiz 139
Question 9

Quiz 141
More Horror

Questions	Answers
1 Who played Dracula in the spoof horror, *Dracula: Dead and Loving It*?	*Leslie Nielsen*
2 Joshua, Michael and Heather are the main characters in which 1999 horror flick?	**The Blair Witch Project**
3 Which series of horror flicks feature an evil character known as Pinhead?	**Hellraiser**
4 Which 1983 movie, based on a novel, tells the story of a car possessed with an evil spirit?	**Christine**
5 In which 1985 comedy horror did Michael J. Fox play a werewolf?	**Teenwolf**
6 In which 1999 movie is Johnny Depp terrorized by a headless horseman?	**Sleepy Hollow**
7 What is the title of the 1997 sequel to *An American Werewolf in London*?	**An American Werewolf in Paris**
8 Who plays the title role in the horror *Dracula 2000*?	*Gerard Butler*
9 Which 1979 movie with James Brolin featured the occupants of a haunted house?	**The Amityville Horror**
10 Who played the possessed child Regan in the horror classic *The Exorcist*?	*Linda Blair*

Quiz 142
Question 3

Questions	Answers
1 Which 1987 thriller featured a married couple called Dan and Beth Gallagher?	Fatal Attraction
2 In which movie is Jodie Foster terrorized by three intruders at her New York home?	Panic Room
3 Which 1991 thriller featured an evil nanny called Peyton Flanders?	The Hand that Rocks the Cradle
4 Who played a police detective in the crime thrillers *Seven* and *Kiss the Girls*?	*Morgan Freeman*
5 Which action thriller features Vinnie Jones and Nicholas Cage as a pair of car thieves?	Gone in 60 Seconds
6 What is the name of the CIA agent played by Harrison Ford in *Patriot Games*?	*Jack Ryan*
7 Which 1999 psychological thriller featured Bruce Willis and Samuel L. Jackson?	Unbreakable
8 In which 1972 movie did Burt Reynolds and Jon Voight embark on a nightmare canoe trip?	Deliverance
9 Who connects the thrillers *Spy Game, Three Days of the Condor* and *Legal Eagles*?	*Robert Redford*
10 In which movie did Will Smith play Robert Dean, a lawyer who is framed for murder?	Enemy of the State

Quiz 141
Question 2

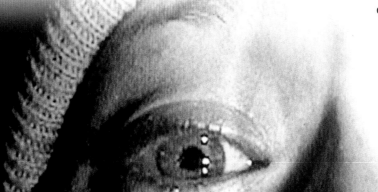

Quiz 143
Michael Caine

Questions	Answers
1 What is Caine's real name?	*Maurice Micklewhite*
2 He took his stage surname from which comedy starring Humphrey Bogart?	**The Caine Mutiny**
3 In which 1988 comedy did Caine and Steve Martin play a pair of conmen?	**Dirty Rotten Scoundrels**
4 In which acclaimed drama did Caine play the role of Dr. Wilbur Larch?	**The Cider House Rules**
5 In which 1998 movie did he co-star with Jane Horrocks?	**Little Voice**
6 Which movie starring Caine was about a plot to assassinate Winston Churchill?	**The Eagle has Landed**
7 Which Camden pop group had a hit with a song entitled "Michael Caine"?	*Madness*
8 Name the star who played the title role in a 2000 remake of the 1971 movie *Get Carter*.	*Sylvester Stallone*
9 Who did Caine play in *The Muppets Christmas Carol*?	*Ebenezer Scrooge*
10 What rank was the character played by Caine in the movie *Zulu*?	*Lieutenant*

Quiz 144
Question 8

Quiz 144
Question 3

Quiz 144
Frank Sinatra

Questions	Answers
1 Who played Sinatra in the 1998 biopic, *The Rat Pack*?	*Ray Liotta*
2 Which 1953 movie earned Sinatra an Oscar for his portrayal of Sergeant Maggio?	**From Here to Eternity**
3 Which movie starring Sinatra and Bing Crosby was a parody of the Robin Hood story?	**Robin and the Seven Hoods**
4 Which "rat pack" movie of 1960 was remade in 2001 starring George Clooney?	**Ocean's Eleven**
5 Who was Sinatra married to from 1951 to 1954?	*Ava Gardner*
6 In which 1965 war movie did he play a prisoner killed trying to escape on a train?	**Von Ryan's Express**
7 Which capital city provides the surname for the detective played by Sinatra in 1965?	*Rome – Tony Rome*
8 In which 1956 musical did he sing the song, "Adelaide"?	**Guys and Dolls**
9 What 1963 movie saw Sinatra bound for the second largest state in the U.S.A.?	**Four For Texas**
10 Which Sinatra sang the theme song of the James Bond movie *You Only Live Twice*?	*Nancy Sinatra – his daughter*

Quiz 143
Question 9

Quiz 143
Question 6

Quiz 145
Doctor Zhivago

Questions	Answers
1 In which country is *Doctor Zhivago* set?	*Russia*
2 Who directed the picture?	*David Lean*
3 In which country was the star of the movie, *Omar Sharif*, born?	*Egypt*
4 On whose novel was *Doctor Zhivago* based?	*Boris Pasternak*
5 What is the first name of Doctor Zhivago?	*Yuri*
6 Which British star played Lara in *Doctor Zhivago*?	*Julie Christie*
7 During which war was the movie set?	*World War I*
8 Who played General Zhivago in the movie?	*Alec Guinness*
9 In what year of the 1960s was the picture released?	*1965*
10 What is the first name of the character played by Geraldine Chaplin?	*Tonya*

Quiz 146
Question 8

Quiz 146
Question 4

Quiz 146
West Side Story

Questions	Answers
1 On which Shakespeare play was *West Side Story* based?	**Romeo and Juliet**
2 Who played the leading lady Maria in the movie?	*Natalie Wood*
3 In which year of the 1960s was the movie made?	*1961*
4 In *West Side Story* what is the name of the rival gang of the Sharks?	*The Jets*
5 Who composed the music for the movie?	*Leonard Bernstein*
6 In which city is *West Side Story* set?	*New York*
7 Who won a Best Supporting Actor Oscar for his portrayal of the gang leader Riff?	*George Chakaris*
8 Which song contains the line, "I like the city of San Juan. I know a boat you can get on"?	*"America"*
9 How many Oscars did *West Side Story* win?	*Ten*
10 Whose singing voice does the soprano Marnie Nixon overdub?	*Natalie Wood's*

Quiz 145
Question 3

Quiz 145
Question 1

Quiz 147

In The Back Row

Questions	Answers
1 Which 2003 movie sees Nick Nolte playing the father of Dr. Bruce Banner?	Hulk
2 Which actor was America's most decorated soldier of World War II?	*Audie Murphy*
3 Who played the writer Joan Wilder in both *Romancing the Stone* and *Jewel of the Nile*?	*Kathleen Turner*
4 In which movie did Jennifer Grey play the character of Baby Houseman?	Dirty Dancing
5 Elliot Carver is the name of the villain in which *Bond* movie?	Tomorrow Never Dies
6 Which 1990 movie features Leonardo, Michelangelo, Donatello and Raphael?	Teenage Mutant Ninja Turtles
7 In which 1982 comedy did Dustin Hoffman play the characters of Michael and Dorothy?	Tootsie
8 Which singing legend played the owner of a beauty salon in *Steel Magnolias*?	*Dolly Parton*
9 In which movie did Elton John sing "Pinball Wizard"?	Tommy
10 Who plays the role of Leo Getz in the *Lethal Weapon* movies?	*Joe Pesci*

Quiz 148
Question 6

Quiz 148

Preview

Questions	Answers
1 Which 1995 movie saw Ted Danson searching for a Scottish monster?	Loch Ness
2 Who played the central character in the 1968 version of *Planet of the Apes*?	*Charlton Heston*
3 Which American wrestler plays the title role in the 2002 movie *The Scorpion King*?	*The Rock – Dwayne Johnson*
4 Which *Carry On* star became the landlady of The Queen Vic in *EastEnders*?	*Barbara Windsor*
5 In a 1984 movie, who did Linda Lee turn into when donning a red cape?	*Supergirl*
6 In the *Stuart Little* movies what kind of animal was Stuart Little?	A white mouse
7 Which 1984 gangster flick was based on a novel called *The Hoods*?	Once Upon a Time in America
8 Who played the Martian in the 1999 picture *My Favorite Martian*?	*Christopher Lloyd*
9 Which sleuth did Margaret Rutherford portray in the thriller *Murder Most Foul*?	*Miss Marple*
10 Who plays the role of Zed in the *Men in Black* movies?	*Rip Torn*

Quiz 147
Question 6

Quiz 149
Movie Buffs

Questions	Answers
1 Which star's first name means "fresh breeze coming down from the mountains"?	*Keanu Reeves*
2 Bert and Ernie from *Sesame Street* were named after characters from which movie?	*It's a Wonderful Life*
3 In *The Thirty-Nine Steps*, who has been played by Robert Powell and Kenneth More?	*Richard Hannay*
4 Which 1930s movie was the first picture to have its sequel released in the same year?	*King Kong, both made in 1933*
5 Which Oscar winner holds the title of "Baron of Richmond upon Thames"?	*Richard Attenborough*
6 Which star said, "If I'd have known that, I'd have put on an eye patch 35 years ago"?	*John Wayne*
7 Who connects *The Swiss Family Robinson*, *The Vikings* and *King of Kings*?	*All narrated by Orson Welles*
8 Who became the first star to win an Oscar for a performance in a foreign language?	*Sophia Loren*
9 Which star of *Coronation Street* went on to become an Oscar-winning actor?	*Ben Kingsley*
10 What was used to simulate blood in Alfred Hitchcock's *Psycho*?	*Chocolate syrup*

Quiz 150
Question 10

Quiz 150
Question 9

Quiz 150

Tough Trivia

Questions	Answers
1 The Black Maria is the name of the world's first-ever movie studio. Who founded it?	*Thomas Alva Edison*
2 In what year was *The Alamo* set?	*1836*
3 In what capacity did Bombardier Billy Wells appear at the beginning of many pictures?	*He banged the Rank gong*
4 In the world of movie making what is a martini shot?	*The last shot of a day's filming*
5 How did Alfred Hitchcock make his usual cameo appearance in the movie *Life Boat*?	*In an advert for weight loss*
6 What Oscar first was achieved by Julius J. Epstein and Philip G. Epstein in 1943?	*First Oscar-winning twins*
7 Who played Jesus in *The Greatest Story Ever Told* and the Devil in *Needful Things*?	*Max von Sydow*
8 Which actor renamed himself after his hometown of Gary, Indiana?	*Gary Cooper*
9 In which movie did Gene Hackman provide the voice of General Mandible?	**Antz**
10 Which actress played Virginia Wolf in *The Hours*?	*Nicole Kidman*

Quiz 149
Question 10

Quiz 149
Question 2

Quiz 151
The Final Curtain

Questions	Answers
1 Who died in 1984 and is famous for his numerous portrayals of Tarzan?	*Johnny Weismuller*
2 Which legend died in 1977 and was later played on screen by Faye Dunaway?	*Joan Crawford*
3 Who played Q for the last time in the Bond movie *The World is not Enough*?	*Desmond Llewelyn*
4 Which actor's 1999 funeral was attended by Alex Higgins and Richard Harris?	*Oliver Reed*
5 Which founder member of United Artists was born Gladys Smith and died in 1979?	*Mary Pickford*
6 The 1971 biography *Other Side of the Rainbow* is about which movie legend?	*Judy Garland*
7 Whose last screen performance came in *The Hunter* as bounty-hunter Papa Thorson?	*Steve McQueen*
8 Who made his final appearance in the 1964 movie *The Killers*?	*Ronald Reagan*
9 Who died first, Bud Abbot or Lou Costello?	*Lou Costello – in 1959*
10 *Horror Man* is the biography of which actor?	*Boris Karloff*

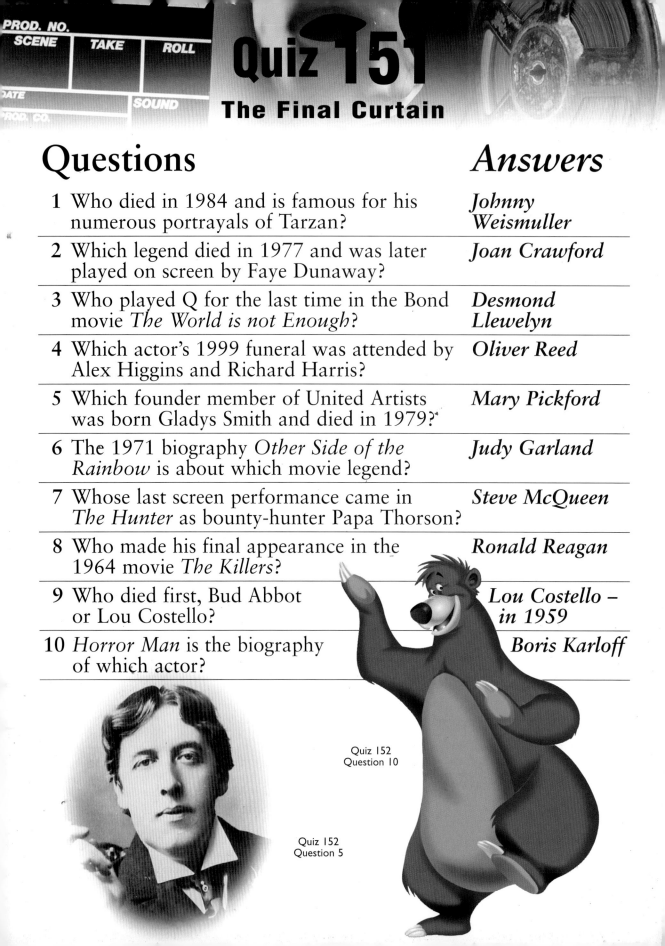

Quiz 152
Question 10

Quiz 152
Question 5